THE SONGS AND MUSIC

INTERNATIONAL EDUCATION SERIES

THE SONGS AND MUSIC

OF FRIEDRICH FROEBEL'S MOTHER PLAY

(MUTTER UND KOSE LIEDER)

SONGS NEWLY TRANSLATED AND FURNISHED WITH NEW MUSIC

PREPARED AND ARRANGED BY

SUSAN E. BLOW

"Deep meaning oft lies hid in childish play"
SCHILLKR

GYAN

Published by

Gyan Publishing House
5, Ansari Road
Daryaganj, New Delhi-110002
Phone: 011-47034999, 9811692060
E-mail: books@gyanbooks.com

Distribution Network
gyanbooks.com
India, USA, Canada, UK, Australia, France

ISBN : 978-81-212-6292-7 (PB)
First Published, 1895

2nd Impression 2022

Printed at: Gyan Press, Delhi.

THE SONGS AND MUSIC
Author: FRIEDRICH FROEBEL'S

INTERNATIONAL EDUCATION SERIES

THE SONGS AND MUSIC

OF FRIEDRICH FROEBEL'S MOTHER PLAY

(MUTTER UND KOSE LIEDER)

SONGS NEWLY TRANSLATED AND FURNISHED WITH NEW MUSIC

PREPARED AND ARRANGED BY

SUSAN E. BLOW

"Deep meaning oft lies hid in childish play"

SCHILLER

EDITOR'S PREFACE.

THE publishers have divided this work of Froebel in order to bring it into volumes of convenient size. The edition of Wichard Lange and the former English translations have the form and style of a music book. In separating the contents for this division, the mottoes, commentaries, and mother communings have been placed in the first volume, which may be called the Mother's volume. The songs and music are reserved for the present volume, which is the Children's volume. What it contains is suitable for children's ears and voices.

As already mentioned in the preface to the first volume, the illustrations are reproduced from the large and well-executed cuts of the Wichard Lange edition, long since out of print, and now very difficult to procure even from an antiquarian bookstore. The pictures in that edition are large enough (6 by 9 inches) to show the minute details. In order to preserve these details the publishers of the present edition (size of page 3⅛ by 5 inches) have been at the pains of repeating and enlarging the parts of certain of the pictures, making in some cases two or three new pictures, and bringing out what is obscure with greater distinctness than is found even in the Lange edition. Inasmuch as the children are expected to find all these particulars in their study of the illustrations, and trace out the motives of the artist, this feature of the work will be appreciated by all kindergartners.

The publishers have also enlarged the Lange pictures to four times the size of the original, and printed them on a series of charts for use in the kindergartens, furnishing them at a moderate price.

The new music herewith offered will justify itself as a substitute for that which has been discarded.

I have already stated in my preface to the former volume the reasons that have made it desirable to obtain new and more poetic translations of these Froebelian songs. I have gone so far as to say that "most of the literal imitations of Froebel's poetry have contributed in a greater or less degree to ruin the poetic sense of teachers and pupils." I believe that I shall be sustained in this opinion by all kindergartners possessed of genuine poetic taste, but I think that the versions here offered will be found sure to commend themselves to all who have a "literary conscience."

W. T. HARRIS.

WASHINGTON, D. C., *October, 1895.*

MISS BLOW'S PREFACE.

THE poems in this volume are not literal translations of those in the original Mother Play, but attempts to cast Froebel's ideas into truly poetic form. A few songs have been added, in order to develop the thoughts suggested in some of the more important plays, and a series of Wandering Games has been given to illustrate Froebel's method of genetic evolution. A full account of the development of these games, under Froebel's own guidance, will be found in the Pedagogics of the Kindergarten, pages 247–254.*

Since most of the melodies in the original Mother Play have been condemned by competent critics, new music is given in this volume. This music consists in part of melodies written by composers of acknowledged merit, and in part of selections from folk-songs. A few of the best melodies in the original Mother Play have been retained, and, finally, some of the music of Karl Reinecke has been used.

Grateful acknowledgments are due to Miss Eleanor Smith, and to her publishers (Messrs. Milton Bradley and Thomas Charles), for per-

* International Education Series, vol. xxx.

mission to use eight songs from Volume I and one song from Volume II of her Songs for Little Children. Miss Smith's books contain songs on all the subjects omitted in this volume (Good Morning Songs, Weather Songs, Songs of the Seasons, Christmas, Easter, and Thanksgiving Songs, Flower Songs, Gift Songs, Patriotic Songs, etc.); and I earnestly hope that her interest in and generosity toward the Mother Play may increase the influence of her already well-known and popular collections.

I desire also to express my sincere thanks to Mrs. Emily Huntington Miller for The Little Maiden and The Stars and The Farmyard, as well as for her kindness in adapting The Farmyard, by Mrs. Follen; to Mrs. Eliot for The Cuckoo, Hide and Seek, and The Child's Prayer; to Miss M. J. Garland for the poem and music of Play with the Limbs; to Miss Kate L. Brown for The Finger Piano, and for the use of The Little Plant; to Miss Emilie Poulsson for permission to use her poems Calling the Pigeons and The Weathervane; to Miss Elizabeth C. Le Bourgeois for the poem of The Light-Bird; to Miss Eleonore Heerwart for the use of The Trees; to Mr. W. L. Tomlins for the use of Rippling, Purling Little River; to Oliver Ditson Co. for use of Butterflies; and to Mr. Fred. Field Bullard for generous help in the revision of music.

The folk-songs* in this collection were se-

---

* On pages 161, 162, 172, 174, 176, 186, 202, 204, 207, 209, 211, 217, 228, 240, 243, and 263. Mr. Bullard also wrote the accompaniments to the songs on pages 187, 188, 198, 236, 239, and 257.

lected and adapted to the poems by Miss Euphemia M. Parker, and were arranged for the pianoforte by Mr. Fred. Field Bullard. Of these songs Mr. George L. Osgood writes as follows:

> It is with genuine pleasure I have read the selection of folk-songs made by Miss Euphemia M. Parker and arranged by Mr. Fred. F. Bullard. These quaint old melodies, sprung from the heart of Nature herself, are especially appropriate to the child life of the Froebel verses. The selection shows rare taste and fine instinct, and the accompaniments the trained musician's hand.
>
> GEORGE L. OSGOOD.
>
> BOSTON, MASS., 1895.

Miss Emilie Poulsson's charming volume of Finger Plays is a valuable collateral to the Mother Play. I would call particular attention to The Little Men, The Little Plant, and A Little Boy's Walk, as songs to be used in connection with The Greeting, Naming the Fingers, The Little Gardener, and The Pigeon House.

SUSAN E. BLOW.

CAZENOVIA, N. Y., *Nov. 2, 1895.*

CONTENTS.

SONGS AND GAMES.

SONGS AND PICTURES.

PLAY WITH THE LIMBS.

Up and down, and in and out,
Toss the little limbs about;
Kick the pretty dimpled feet—
That's the way to grow, my sweet!
    This way and that,
    With a pat-a-pat-pat,
    With one, two, three,
    For each little knee.

By-and-bye, in work and play,
They'll be busy all the day;
Wading in the water clear,
Running swift for mother dear.
    So this way and that,
    With a pat-a-pat-pat,
    And one, two, three,
    For each little knee.

Emily Huntington Miller.

Strampfelbein.

Flugs gieb mir das Strampfelbein,
Wollen schlagen aus Mohn und Lein
Oel für 's Lämpchen zierlich, klein,
Das es brenne hell und rein
Wenn Mutterlieb' in langer Nacht
Für 's liebe, kleine Kindchen wacht.

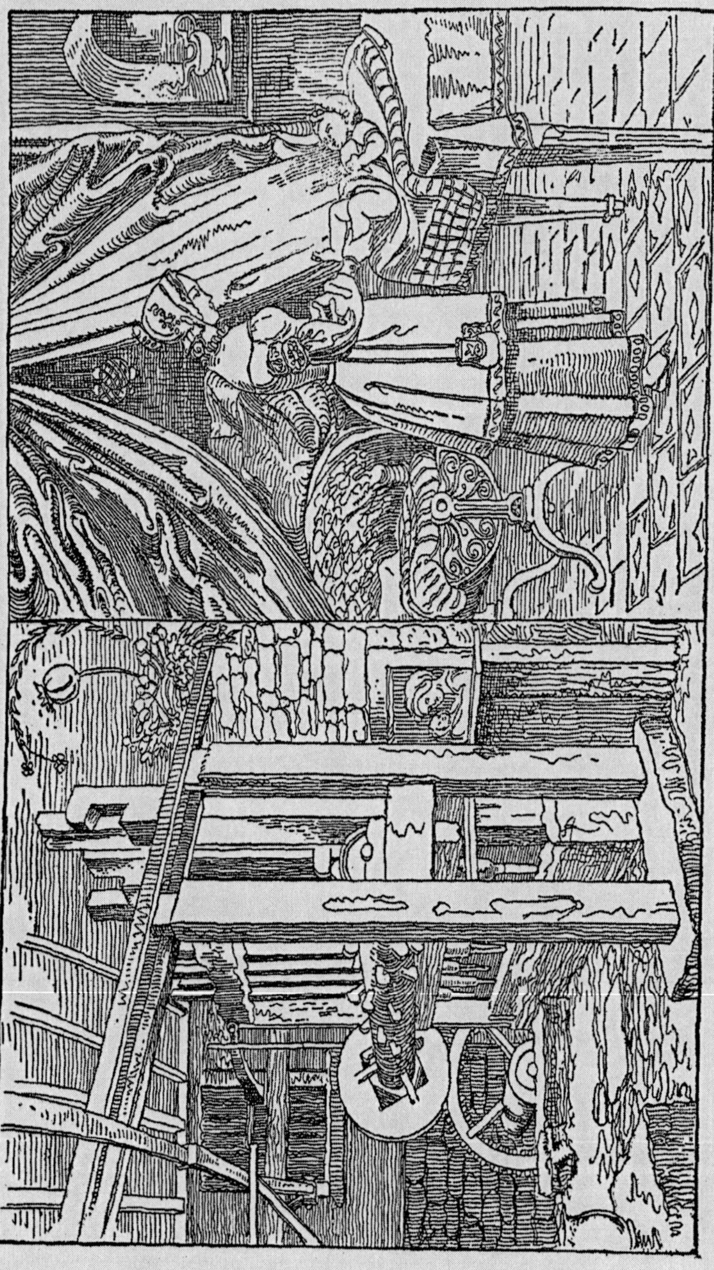

FALLING! FALLING!

DOWN goes baby,
  Mother's pet;
Up comes baby,
  Laughing yet.
Baby well may laugh at harm,
While beneath is mother's arm.

Down goes baby,
  Without fear;
Up comes baby,
  Gaily here.
All is joy for baby while
In the light of mother's smile.

EMILIE POULSSON.

THE WEATHER-VANE.

WEATHERCOCK, what makes you go
Round and round the whole day so?

'Tis the wind whirls me!
'Tis the wind twirls me!
So to all the world I show
How the merry wind doth go.

Pretty kite, what makes you fly,
Up above the tree-tops high?

'Tis the wind lifts me!
'Tis the wind drifts me!
Tosses me in merry play,
Here and there and every way.

Windmill, high on yonder hill,
What makes your sails go turning still?

'Tis the wind loves them!
'Tis the wind moves them!
Helps them turn the mill-stones round,
So your meal and flour's ground.

The wind can do so many things,
The airy sprite on viewless wings:
It waves the flag, it bends the tree,
It shakes our curls for you and me;
And in our merry play we too,
Show all the things the wind can do.

LAURA E. RICHARDS.

THE WEATHER-VANE.

THIS way, that way,
  Turns the weather-vane;
This way, that way,
  Turns and turns again.
Turning, pointing, ever showing,
How the merry wind is blowing.

EMILIE POULSSON.

Das Thurmhähnchen.

Wie das Hähnchen auf dem Thurme
Sich kann drehn im Wind und Sturme,
Kann mein Kind sein Händchen wenden,
So sich neue Freuden spenden.

ALL GONE!

All gone! the supper's gone!
White bread and milk so sweet,
For baby dear to eat.
All gone! the supper's gone!
Where did baby's supper go?
Tongue, you had a share, I know.
Little mouth, with open lips,
Through your rosy gate it slips.
Little throat, you know full well
Where it went, if you would tell.
Little hands, grow strong;
Little legs, grow long;
Little cheeks, grow red:
You have all been fed.

Emily Huntington Miller.

'S ist all-all.

All-all! mein Kind, all-all!
Das Süppchen ist nun all.
Ei! wo ist 's denn hingekommen?—
Mündchen hat 's zu sich genommen,
Züng'chen hat 's zurück gedruckt,
Kehlchen hat 's hinabgeschluckt,
Mäglein hat es schon verdaut,
Noch vom Zähnlein nicht gekaut.
Drum ist mein Kind auch wohlgemuth,
Und weiß und roth, wie Milch und Blut!

TASTE SONG.

WHEN the red lips open wide,
And you part the teeth inside,
Then a tiny door you show,
Where this little plum may go.
Now the pink tongue comes in haste,
All the pleasant juice to taste.
Ah, 'tis very nice and sweet!
Fruit like this is good to eat.

Bid good-bye to juicy plum;
Let the sour apple come—
Take a dainty little bite
From its cheek all red and white.
What a funny face you make!
How your little head you shake!
In your look I see confessed
That you like the sweet things best.

Now the bitter almond try,
Brown its shell, and hard and dry;
Yet within, a kernel white
Shyly hides away from sight.
Yes, it draws the mouth a bit,
But it's wholesome, every whit.
Many bitter things you'll meet:
Time, perhaps, will make them sweet.

All the fruits and nuts, in turn,
Teach a lesson you may learn.
If a thing is ripe all through,
Then 'tis very good for you;
But to eat the unripe things,
Sharpest pain and trouble brings;
Though they look so fresh and fair,
Danger, dear, is hiding there.

NORA ARCHIBALD SMITH.

FLOWER SONG.

SMELL the flower, my child, and see
What its perfume tells to thee.
In its cup, so small and bright,
Safely hidden from our sight,
There an angel-spirit dwells,
And its message sweetly tells.

"From my tender resting-place,
Little one with happy face,
I am talking to thee, dear,
Though no voice my child may hear;
But my perfume sweet will tell,
Little friend, I love thee well."

KATE L. BROWN.

TICK! TACK!

SWING, swong! this is the way
Goes the pendulum night and day.
"Tick! tock! tick! tock!"
Never resting, says the clock.
"Time for work and time for fun,
Time to sleep when day is done.
Tick! tock!" Hear the clock!
"Time to rest each little head;
Time the children were in bed."

Swing, swong! sure and slow
Goes the pendulum to and fro.
"Tick! tock! tick! tock!"
In the morning says the clock.
"Time to wake from slumber sweet,
Time to wash and time to eat.
Tick! tock!" Hear the clock,
"Tick, tack, tock!" it cries,
"Children, it is time to rise!"

EMILY HUNTINGTON MILLER.

Tick, Tack!

Sehet nur, sehet nur!
Wie der Pendel an der Uhr,
Geht das Aermchen hin und her,
Doch nicht kreuz und doch nicht quer;
Denn es gehet Schlag bei Schlag,
Immer tick und immer tack.
Tick, tack; tick, tack.—
Uhr, mach' mir nur ja kein Leid,
Zeig' mir immer richt'ge Zeit:
Zum Essen, zum Schlafen, zum Zeitvertreib,
Zum Waschen und Baden den ganzen Leib;
Denn mein Herzchen will stets rein,
Will gesund und thätig sein.
Aermchen, geh' drum Schlag bei Schlag,
Immer tick und immer tack.
Tick, tack; tack.

MOWING GRASS.

PETER, Peter, quickly go
To the field the grass to mow;
Juicy grass, and hay so sweet,
Bring them for the cow to eat.
Lina, Lina, milk the cow;
Good milk she will give us now.
Milk to drink, with rolls or bread,
Thus we little ones are fed.

Let us thank our friends, each one:
Peter, for the mowing done,
Lina, for the milking, too,
And for milk, good cow, thank *you*.
Thanks to all are gladly said:
Baker, thank you for the bread.
Thanks dear mother shall not miss,
Given with a loving kiss.

EMILIE POULSSON.

Grasmähen.

Peter! gehe auf die Wiese,
Mähe schnell das Gras, das süße;
Bringe heim das gute Futter,
Für die Küh' zu Milch und Butter.
Lenchen! milch die Küh' als-
balde,
Bring' die Milch ohn' Auf-
enthalte;
Kuh muß ja die Milch uns reichen
Zu den guten Semmelbreichen,
Daß das Kindchen sich recht labe,
An so vieler will'gen Gabe.—
Peter! gehe auf die Wiese,
Mähe schnell das Gras, das süße.
Danke Dir dann für Dein Mähen,
Und der Kuh für's Milchher-
geben;
Dann der Lenchen für das Milch-
en,
Auch dem Bäcker für's Semmel-
chen,
Und der Mutter für den Brei,
Daß kein Dank vergessen sei.

THE RHYME OF THE BOWL OF MILK.

Oh, here is the milk, so sweet and white,
All ready for dear little baby!

This is the mother, who with delight
Poured into the bowl the milk so white,
All ready for dear little baby!

This is the milkmaid, who worked with a will
Her pail with the cow's good milk to fill,
To take to the mother, who with delight
Poured into the bowl the milk so white,
All ready for dear little baby!

This is the cow that gave milk each day
To Molly the milkmaid, who worked with a will
Her pail with the cow's good milk to fill,
To take to the mother, who with delight
Poured into the bowl the milk so white,
All ready for dear little baby!

This is the dry and sweet-smelling hay
That was fed to the cow that gave milk each day
To Molly, the milkmaid, who worked with a will
Her pail with the cow's good milk to fill,
To take to the mother, who with delight
Poured into the bowl the milk so white,
All ready for dear little baby!

This is the grass—(in the field it grew,
Helped by the sunshine, and rain, and dew)—
The grass that was dried into sweet-smelling hay,
And fed to the cow that gave milk each day
To Molly, the milkmaid, who worked with a will
Her pail with the cow's good milk to fill,
To take to the mother, who with delight
Poured into the bowl the milk so white,
All ready for dear little baby!

This is the mower, who worked at the farm,
Swinging the scythe with his strong right arm,
Mowing the fields of grass that grew,
Helped by the sunshine, and rain, and dew—
The grass that was dried into sweet-smelling hay.
And fed to the cow that gave milk each day
To Molly, the milkmaid, who worked with a will
Her pail with the cow's good milk to fill,
To take to the mother, who with delight
Poured into the bowl the milk so white,
All ready for dear little baby!

EMILIE POULSSON.

BECKONING THE CHICKENS.

TINY fingers in a row,
Beckon to the chickens—so.
Downy little chickens dear,
Fingers say, "Come here! come here!"
  Chick! chick! chick! chick!
Fingers say, "Come here! come here!"
Pretty chickens, soft and small,
Do not fear—we love you all!

EMILY HUNTINGTON MILLER.

Hühnchenwinken.
Wink' den Hühnchen, daß sie kommen,
Sag': „Ihr seid mir schön willkommen."

Täubchenwinken.

Die Täubchen *) wollen zum Kindchen kommen;
Wink' ihnen und sag': „Seid schön mir willkommen."

*) Vöglein.

BECKONING THE PIGEONS.

CALL the pigeons, baby dear—
  Beckon them to you;
Hear them answer lovingly,
  Coo-oo! coo-oo! coo!

EMILIE POULSSON.

BECKONING THE PIGEONS.

SEE the pretty pigeons, coming, love, to meet
  you!
Little dimpled hand, can you learn to say, "I
  greet you?"
Bend the rosy fingers, wave them to and fro:
Pigeons, pretty pigeons, baby greets you so.

Smooth your shining feathers, spread your glossy
  wings;
Baby loves to see you, gentle, fearless things.
Here is grain to feed you, but, before you fly,
Pigeons, pretty pigeons, baby says "Good-bye!"

EMILY HUNTINGTON MILLER.

THE FISH IN THE BROOK.

MERRY little fishes,
 In the brook at play,
Floating in the shallows,
 Darting swift away.
"Happy little fishes, come and play with me!"
"No, O no!" the fishes say, "that can never be!"

Pretty bodies curving,
 Bending like a bow,
Through the clear, bright water,
 See them swiftly go.
"Happy little fishes, may we play with you?"
"No, O no!" the fishes say, "that would never do!"

EMILY HUNTINGTON MILLER.

Die Fischlein.

Lustig im klaren Bächlein
Spielen die kleinen Fischlein:
Sie schwimmen darinnen immer herum,
Bald sind sie g'rad, und bald sind sie krumm.

THE TARGET.

ONE piece this way,
  And one piece that,
And a smooth little board
  That is round and flat.
Drive in a peg
  That will hold them well,
And here is a target,
  Ready to sell!
"What costs it?" "Three halfpennies."
  "That is too dear;
Only two halfpennies
  Have I here."
"Three halfpennies is just enough—
One for the work and two for the stuff.
Three halfpennies the buyer must pay;
Who can not pay it must run away."

EMILY HUNTINGTON MILLER.

PAT-A-CAKE.

COME, my baby, you shall make
Mother dear a little cake.
Roll it this way, roll it that,
Pat the cake all smooth and flat;
Mark it there, and mark it here—
There's a cake for mother dear.

Baker, is your oven hot?
Bake my cake, but burn it not.
Here's the oven, hot and ready,
Toss the cake in, straight and steady.
Bake it brown, and bring it here,
Baby's cake for mother dear.

EMILY HUNTINGTON MILLER.

Patsche-Kuchen.

Kindchen! wollen es versuchen,
Uns zu backen einen Kuchen:
Patsche, patsch' den Kuchen glatt,
Der Bäcker sagt: „Nun ist es satt;
Bringt mir doch den Kuchen bald,
Sonst wird ja der Ofen kalt.“—
„„Bäcker! hier ist mein Kuchen fein,
Back' ihn schön für mein Kindchen klein.““
„Bald soll der Kuchen gebacken sein,
Tief in den Ofen schieb' ich ihn ein.“

THE NEST.

Here's a pretty cradle nest,
  Snug, and warm, and round;
Cuddled in the downy bed,
  Little nestling birds we found.
    "Stay! stay!" the birdies say,
    "Mother, do not fly away!"
    "Dear, so dear, never fear!
    Mother waits and watches near."
    Peep! peep! Dear, so dear,
    Hush, my babies, do not fear!"

Emily Huntington Miller.

Vogelnest.

In die Hecke, auf die Aestchen
Baut der Vogel sich ein Nestchen;
Legt hinein zwei Eierlein,
Brütet draus zwei Vögelein;
Rufen die Mutter: „Pip, pip, pip!
Mütterchen, Du bist uns lieb!“

THE FLOWER-BASKET.

WEAVE the little basket, fill it up with posies,
  Roses from the garden, blossoms from the wood.
With our birthday wishes, with our songs and kisses,
  Bring it to the father, dear and kind and good.
    With smiles and with singing
    Our gift we are bringing,
    But love is the treasure
    We give without measure.

EMILY HUNTINGTON MILLER.

Blumenkörbchen.

Kindchen! woll'n ein Körbchen machen,
D'rin zu tragen schöne Sachen:
Blümchen woll'n wir darin tragen,
Werden drob sich nicht beklagen,
Wollen sie dem Vater bringen,
Ihm ein Liedchen dazu singen:
La, la; la, la; lieb Blümelein,
Sollt nun bei dem Vater sein;
La, la; la, la; la, la; la, la.

THE PIGEON-HOUSE.

OH, see my pigeon-house so high!
Come, my pretty pigeons, haste to fly!
  To pleasant fields they swiftly go,
  So busy gleaning to and fro,
And when they come back to rest at night,
Again I close my pigeon-house tight.

Here, in the home so snug and warm,
Live the little children safe from harm.
  They pass the day in merry play,
  Through woods and meadows green they stray,
But when they come back at night to rest,
Father and mother and home are best.

When evening shadows slowly creep,
Softly coo the pigeons, nestling to sleep.
  The gentle mother, wise and dear,
  Her happy children gathers near,
And sings to the baby on her breast,
"The world is pleasant, but home is best."

EMILY HUNTINGTON MILLER.

Das Taubenhaus.

Ich öffne jetzt mein Taubenhaus,
Die Täubchen fliegen froh hinaus;
Sie fliegen hin auf 's grüne Feld,
Wo 's ihnen gar zu wohl gefällt.
Doch kehr'n sie heim zu guter Ruh,
So schließ' ich wieder mein Häuschen zu.

NAMING THE FINGERS.

THIS is little Tommy Thumb,
Round and smooth as any plum.
This is busy Peter Pointer;
Surely he's a double-jointer.
This is mighty Toby Tall;
He's the biggest one of all.
This is dainty Reuben Ring;
He's too fine for anything.
And this little wee one, maybe,
Is the pretty Finger-baby.
All the five we've counted now,
Busy fingers in a row.
Every finger knows the way
How to work and how to play;
Yet together work they best,
Each one helping all the rest.

LAURA E. RICHARDS.

Das Däumchen ein Pfläumchen.

Dieß ist das runde **Däumchen,**
Es steht aus wie Pfläumchen.
Dieß **Fingerchen** gerade **zeigt,**
Doch aber auch gar schön sich neigt.
Dieß **Fingerchen** das größte ist,
Obgleich es nur zu **mittelst** ist.
Dieß **Fingerchen** trägt 's Ringelein,
Drum ist es auch wie **Gold** so rein.
Dieß **Fingerchen** das **kleinste** ist,
Die Fingerzahl gar fein beschließt.
Und wie verschieden nun auch ihre Gaben sind,
So sind sie einig doch beisammen, liebes Kind.

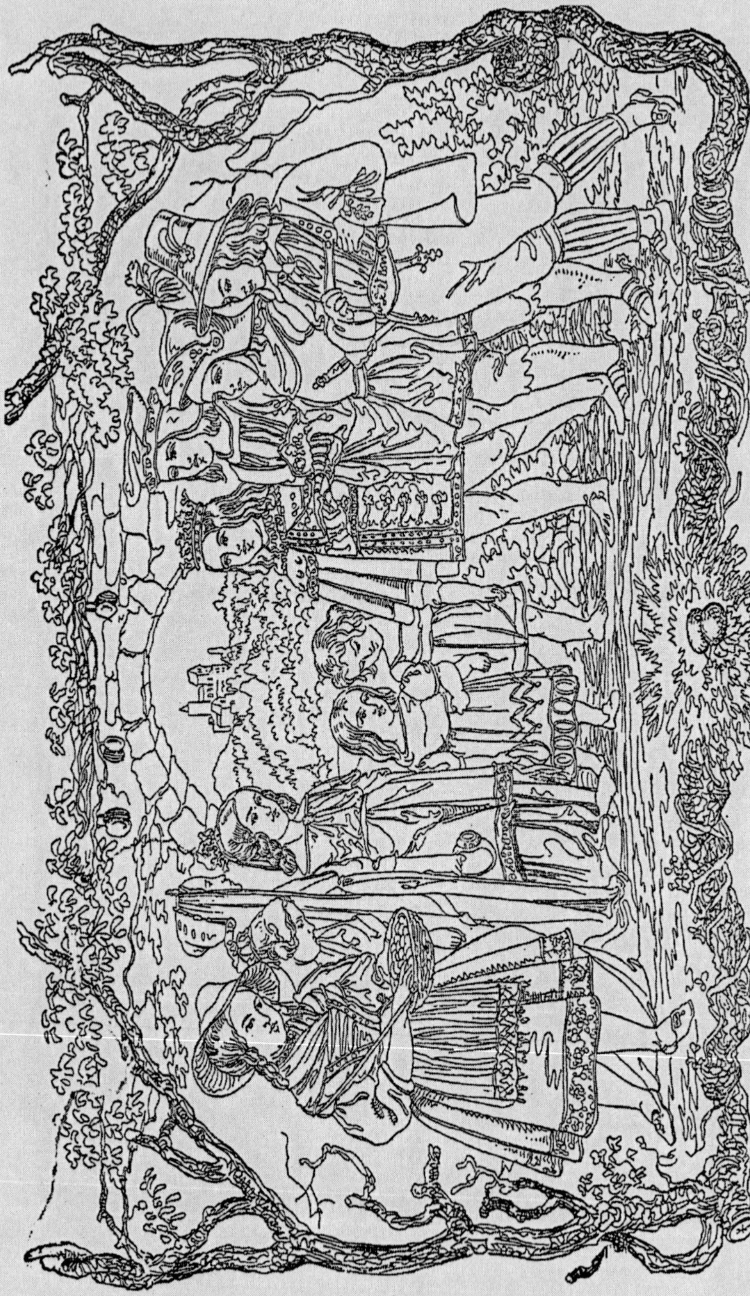

5

THE GREETING.

Now see them here,
These friends so dear,
As they together meet;
With bows polite,
And faces bright,
Each other they will greet:
"Oh, how do you do?
And how do you do?
And how do you do again?
And how do you do?
And how do you do?"
Say all these children ten.

EMILIE POULSSON.

Däumchen, neig' dich.

Du **Däumchen** neig' dich,
Du **Zeiger** streck' dich,
Du **Mittler** buck' dich,
Du **Goldner** heb' dich,
Du **Kleiner** duck' dich,
Ja, ja! füge dich.
Ihr Alle möget durch zierliches Beugen,
Euch freundlich des Grußes Ehre bezeigen.

THE FAMILY.

THIS is the loving mother,
  Always good and dear;
This is the busy father,
  Brave and full of cheer;
This is the merry brother,
  Grown so strong and tall:
This is the gentle sister,
  This the baby small;
And here they all together meet,
This whole glad family complete.

EMILIE POULSSON.

Die Großmama und Mutter lieb und gut.

Das ist die Großmama,
Das ist der Großpapa,
Das ist der Vater,
Das ist die Mutter,
Das ist's kleine Kindchen ja;
Seht die ganze Familie da.

Das ist die Mutter, lieb und gut;
Das ist der Vater mit frohem Muth;
Das ist der Bruder, lang und groß;
Das ist die Schwester, mit Püppchen im Schooß;
Und dieß ist das Kindchen, noch klein und zart,
Und dieß die Familie von guter Art,
Die mit sinn'ger, einträchtiger Kraft
Das Rechte und Gute in Freuden schafft.

THE FAMILY.

This is the mother, so busy at home,
Who loves her dear children, whatever may
come.

This is the father, so brave and so strong,
Who works for his family all the day long.

This is the brother, who'll soon be a man;
He helps his good mother as much as he can.

This is the sister, so gentle and mild,
Who plays that the dolly is her little child.

This is the baby, all dimpled and sweet;
How soft his wee hands and his chubby pink feet!

Father, and mother, and children so dear,
Together you see them, one family here.

EMILIE POULSSON.

NUMBERING THE FINGERS.

THE thumb is one,
The pointer two,
The middle finger three!
Ring finger four,
Little finger five,
And that is all, you see.

Now we have put them all to bed,
A quiet sleep to take,
And softly sing a lullaby,
Lest they too early wake.

Lullaby, lullaby, lullaby,
All hushed and still the birdies sit
Upon the branches high.
The flow'rets hang their pretty heads,
The wind sings lullaby,
Lullaby, lullaby, lullaby.

EMILIE POULSSON.

Beim Däumchen sag' ich Eins.

Beim Däumchen sag' ich Eins,
Beim Zeigefinger: Zwei,
Beim Mittelfinger: Drei,
Beim Ringfinger: Vier,
Beim kleinen Finger Fünf ich sage.
Hab' in 's Bettchen all' gelegt,
Schlafen, keines sich mehr regt;
Still, das keins zu früh erwache.

THE FINGER PIANO.

LISTEN, children dear,
The lovely music hear;
Little fingers downward go—
Hark! the answer, sweet and low:
La! la! la! etc.

Rippling, sparkling in the sun,
See the laughing brooklets run.
Tell us, brooklet, in your play,
Tell the song you sing to-day.
Up and down the fingers go,
Brooklets singing as they flow.

Now the merry lark on high
Carols sweetly from the sky;
Wide he spreads his fluttering wings,
Showering gladness as he sings.
Up and down the fingers go;
'Tis the lark's song here below.

Thus the hand, so small a thing,
Still may sweetest music bring.
Fingers, you must move along,
You may help to make the song.
Up and down the fingers go,
Waken, music, sweet and low!

KATE L. BROWN.

Liedchen dazu.

Fröhlich spielt mein Kind allein,
Singt ihm doch ein Liedchen fein.

Sinnig spielt mein Herz in Ruh,
Singt ihm doch ein Lied dazu.

Finger gehen auf und ab,
Bald in Schritt und bald in Trab.

*

Wie des Lerchleins Lied erklingt,
Gleich es seine Flügel schwingt;
So das Fingerspiel sich regt,
Wenn Gesang das Herz bewegt.

*

Meines Kindchens Fingerlein
Sind noch schwach und sind noch klein;
Dennoch, schaut! schon spielt es schön,
Liedchen will das Spiel erhöh'n.

HAPPY BROTHERS AND SISTERS.

FIVE brothers and sisters,
  Busy all the day;
Light goes, night comes,
  Sleepy now are they.

Say the prayer softly,
  Close the tired eyes:
"May our heavenly Father
  Watch us till we rise!"

Happy, happy children,
  Fast asleep are you.
Drop the head! go to bed!
  We are sleepy too!

LAURA E. RICHARDS.

CHILD'S PRAYER.

HEAVENLY Father, day is done,
And the quiet night begun;
Thou hast kept me through the day,
Keep me through the night, I pray.

And, dear Father, while I share
In thy tender love and care,
Help me every day to be
An obedient child to thee.

HENRIETTA R. ELIOT.*

---

* The following lines are suggested by Mrs. Eliot as an alternative to first stanza of this poem:

Now I lay me down to sleep:
Heavenly Father, wilt thou keep
Me and those I love all night,
For with thee 'tis always light.

Die Geschwister ohne Harm.
Sieh hier die Geschwister ohne Harm,
Sie sinken einander sanft Arm in Arm;
Sind müde von des Tags Geschäfte,
Und wollen sammeln neue Kräfte.
Doch ehe sie nun schlafen ein,
Ihr Leben sie befehlen fein,
Dem Lebensgeber ganz allein,
Der Vater ihnen und Schutz mög' sein;
Dann schlafen sie ein in guter Ruh.
Der für alle wacht,
Hat nun auf sie Acht,
Schliest ihnen dann sanft die Aeuglein
zu;
Nun, Kindchen Du mein, ein Gleiches
auch thu,
Und schlafe, schlafe in süßer Ruh.

THE CHILDREN ON THE TOWER.

Two hands and eight little fingers,
  And two little Grandmothers Thumb.
'Tis long since they met, but they never forget,
  So a-visiting now they come.
"How *do* you do?" and "How *do* you do?"
  With nods and bows they say.
"How *do* you do?" and "How do you *do*?
  And what is the news to-day?"
They tell of their making baskets;
  They tell of eggs in the nest;
They tell the loves of the soft white doves
  That flutter and sink to rest;
They tell of the little fishes
  That wriggle their little tails;
They tell of the baker, the pat-a-cake maker,
  Whose kindness never fails;
They tell of the vane on the steeple,
  How this way and that it goes;
Of Peter the mower, who hour by hour,
  The grass and the clover-top mows.

Die Finger sagen: Auf den
Thurm woll'n wir gehn,
Da kann man gar weit um sich
sehn;
Da ist's so schön, so schön, so
schön!
Die Däumchen sagen: Wir blei-
ben zu Haus,
Wir gehen lieber ins Kirchen-
haus.—
Die Fingerchen steigen den Thurm
hinan,
Daß man sie kaum noch sehen
kann.
Sie steigen so hoch, so hoch,
zu hoch!
Da—fall'n sie in ein
tiefes Loch.

"But all the stories are told now,
  And what, oh, what shall we do?"
"We'll climb the tower this very hour,
  And there admire the view."
Thus cry the children gladly,
  But each little Grandmother Thumb,
She courtesys *so*, and she says "No! no!
  I will not, will not come!
We'll go to church together,
  As good little grandmothers do,
And there we'll wait—but don't be late!—
  Yes, there we'll wait for you.
And while in church we're waiting,
  A little prayer we'll say,
And thanks we'll give for the days we live,
  And thanks for the children gay."

The children climb the tower,
  And up and up they go;
Like fairies small look one and all,
  Still mounting in a row.
Now higher still, and higher,
  With never a fear of a fall,
Till one he stumbles, and one he tumbles,
  And down come toppling all!
And down comes the tower itself, too,
  On top of the church—ah me!
Oh, what a smashing! oh, what a crashing!
  And where can the children be?
See! creeping out from the ruins
  By ones and twos they come;
And, deary me! at last we see
  Each good little Grandmother Thumb.
"Oh, bless us now!" and, "Oh, kiss us now!"
  And, "Listen, my dears, to me:
Another day, whatever you say,
  More careful we all must be!"

LAURA E. RICHARDS.

THE CHILD AND THE MOON.

SEE the moon, baby,
  Riding so high!
Will it come, maybe,
  Down from the sky?
"Moon, come and play now,
  Pray you, with me!"
"Nay, my dear, nay, now—
  That can not be.
In my blue home here
  Always I stay;
Yet while I roam here,
  Dear, we can play.
Silver beams gliding
  Down to your feet,
Seeking and hiding,
  Play with you, sweet!
E'en when above you
  Clouds hide my face,
Still I will love you,
  There in my place.
When the clouds fleeting
  Leave my sky clear,
Bright shines my greeting,
  Loving and dear.
If your part you'll do,
  I will do mine;
Yours, to be good and true;
  Mine, just to shine!"

LAURA E. RICHARDS.

Das Kind und der Mond.

Komm, Kindchen, schau den Mond,
Der dort am Himmel wohnt.
„Komm, Mond, komm doch geschwind
Hierher zum lieben Kind!"
„Wohl käm' ich zu Dir gern,
Doch wohn' ich gar zu fern,
Kann aus dem blauen Haus
Hier oben nicht heraus.
Weil ich kann kommen nicht,
Send' ich mein helles Licht;
Um 's Kindchen zu erfreun,
Schick' ich dem milden Schein;
Und bin ich auch nicht nah,
Bin ich in Lieb' doch da.
Sei, Kindchen, nur recht fromm,
Von Zeit zu Zeit ich komm.
Und freundlich ich dann schicke
Dir meine Liebesblicke;
Wir grüßen uns dann beide,
Gemeinsam uns zur Freude."
„Leb' wohl, leb' wohl! mein Mond
Mit Liebe, Liebe lohnt."

THE CHILD AND THE MOON.

"BRIGHT, round moon in the starry sky,
Sailing above the steeple high,
I am so glad your face to see,
Come from your far-off place to me!"

"Dear little child, if I come to thee,
Who will shine for the ships at sea?
And how will the traveller find his way,
Unless in my far-off place I stay?"

"Bright, round moon, you may shine for all,
Sailing above the steeple tall.
Thanks I give for your friendly light,
Beautiful moon! Good-bye! good-night!"

EMILY HUNTINGTON MILLER.

THE LITTLE BOY AND THE MOON.

PRETTY moon, your face I see
Just above the garden tree.
Are you smiling now for me?—
    Moon so brightly smiling!

Yellow moon, so bright, so near,
In the sky so soft and clear,
I can almost reach you here—
    Moon so softly shining!

Bring the ladder strong and new,
Now I know what I will do:
I will climb and sail with you—
    Moon so slowly sailing!

EMILY HUNTINGTON MILLER.

„Mutter! Mond gehn!“ sprach das Kind auf Mutterarme,
Weit ausstreckend sehnend seine kleinen Arme,
Als am klaren Himmel es den Vollmond sah:
Denn es glaubte sich demselben völlig nah.—
„Eine Leiter müßte sein, zum Mond zu steigen,
Wollten wir so hoch dort oben ihn erreichen!“
Gleich das Kindchen bei der Mutter sicherm Wort
Nach der nahen Schopfe, als der Leiter Ort,
Seine Arme wendet, und vertrauend sagt:
(Denn zum Mond zu gehen ihm gar sehr behagt)
„Leiter holen!“ Und fest war sein Sinn
Zum Besuch des Mond's gewendet hin.

THE LITTLE MAIDEN AND THE STARS.

Now the stars begin to peep
  In the sky, so pure and bright;
Baby soon must go to sleep—
  She must bid the stars good-night.
  Little feet are tired of play;
  Come, my darling, come away!

"See the mother-star, so dear!
  With her little children small!
And the father watching near—
  Pretty stars, I love you all!
  When I shut my eyes to sleep
  All the night your watch you keep.

"Father-star, so big and bright,
  Close beside them do you stay?
Are there posies, red and white,
  In the meadows where they play?
  Do you shake the dreamland tree
  Every night for them and me?

"Mother-star, I wish I knew
  How your babies go to bed;
Do they run as chickens do,
  Hiding every yellow head?
  Do you tuck them, soft and deep,
  In a fleecy cloud to sleep?"

Come, my darling! while you sleep
  On your pillow, soft and white,
Stars will through your window peep,
  Smiling, "*Baby, dear, good-night!*
  Sweetly dream and safely rest
  In your pretty cradle nest!"

EMILY HUNTINGTON MILLER.

"Wohl richtig will Dir deuchten
Der Doppelsterne Leuchten:
Was sie so strahlend zeigen,
Ist ihre Liebe Reigen;
In friedig-freud'gem Handeln
Siehst Du sie stille wandeln.—
Doch schaue auch umher
Der kleinen Sterne Heer,
Der Doppelsterne Kinder,
Sie strahlen zwar wohl minder,
Doch immer hell und rein,
Daß klar die Nacht mög' sein."

THE LIGHT-BIRD.

Child.

O birdie, gleaming on the wall,
    Gleaming,
    Gleaming,
Are you coming when I call,
    Or am I dreaming?

Mother.

    'Tis the light-bird,
    A very bright bird,
That is gleaming on the wall.
    'Tis the light-bird,
    A very bright bird,
But it will not heed your call.

Lichtvöglein an der Wand.
Kind:
Lieb Vögelein! Lieb Vögelein!
Lieb Vöglein an der Wand,
Halt mir doch einmal Stand!
Laß dich doch von mir greifen!
Mußt nicht umher so schweifen!
Lieb Vöglein an der Wand,
Halt mir doch einmal Stand!
Mutter:
Das Vöglein ist nur heller Schein,
Den können nicht greifen die Händchen klein,
Der will mit Aeuglein erfasst nur sein,
Durch sie erfreut er das Herzchen rein.
So ist es im Leben bei vielen Gestalten,
Sie lassen sich fest mit der Hand nicht halten;
Doch fasset sie leicht ein zarterer Sinn,
Und beiden ist es dann hoher Gewinn.

CHILD.

I've seen the moonbeams in the night
    Streaming,
    Streaming,
The little stars that twinkle bright
    Like fireflies seeming.

MOTHER.

    Like the light-bird,
    Like the bright bird,
That is gleaming on the wall—
    Like the light-bird,
    Like the bright bird,
They will not heed your call.

MOTHER AND CHILD.

The sun, the moon, the twinkling stars,
    The rainbow in the skies,
A mother's smile, a father's love,
    We catch them with our eyes;
We can not hold them in our hand,
    Yet from them need not part,
For when we've caught them with our eyes,
    We hold them in our heart.

ELIZABETH CHARLESS LE BOURGEOIS.

THE SHADOW RABBIT.

HEY, the rabbit! ho, the rabbit!
  See, the rabbit on the wall
Pricks his ears, for that's his habit—
  Pricks them up and lets them fall.
    Pretty rabbit, stay, now!
    Come with me and play, now!
No, ah, no! he will not stay;
Up he jumps and springs away.

Now the rabbit sits upright,
Munching grass with all his might.
See him wrinkle up his nose!
What's that for, do you suppose?
    Rabbit, shall I feed you?
  "No, I do not need you!
Rabbits made upon the wall
Feed themselves or not at all."

Das Häschen.

Ei! ein Häschen kommt gegangen
An der Wand daher;
Kindchen! Wollen schnell es fan-
gen,
Doch es läuft gar sehr.
Sieh! Wie 's seine Oehrchen spitzet,
Glaubt, es hör' Etwas.
Wie es jetzt schön aufrecht sitzet,
Speis't sein grunes Gras.
Schau, jetzt rümpft 's sein stumpfes
Näschen
Unser kleines muntres Häschen.—
Jetzt, sich 's ganz darnieder kauert,
Denn es sieht, der Jäger lauert:
Pauf!—der Jäger hat geschossen,
Das hat 's Häschen sehr verdrossen:
Nun ist es davon gesprungen,
Häschens Lied ist ausgesungen.

Down our rabbit cowers now;
Sure, some danger lowers now!
See, the hunter with his gun
Thinks he's going to have some fun.
    Puff! the bullet's flying!
    Is our rabbit dying?
Not a bit, for see him run!
Rabbits, too, can have their fun!

LAURA E. RICHARDS.

THE WOLF.

FROM the dark greenwood,
  From the forest fair,
Up comes a gray wolf,
  Trotting here and there.
See how lank and thin is he!
Hungry must the creature be.
In the wood are berries sweet,
But such things he will not eat.

So he goes a-hunting
  Through the meadows fair,
Sniffing, snuffing,
  Prowling here and there.
Wolf, you shall not bear away
Tender kid or lamb to-day;
For I see the hunter stand
With his trusty gun in hand.

LAURA E. RICHARDS.

Wolf und Schwein.

1. Wolf.

Aus dem dunklen Tannenwald,
Wo des Wildes Aufenthalt,
Steh! kommt auch ein Wolf daher,
Läuft die Kreuz und läuft die Quer:
Hart ihn wohl der Hunger plagt;
Doch, er will nicht Früchte essen,
Möchte gern ein Thierchen fressen;
Darum macht er auf sie Jagd.
Jäger aber will 's nicht leiden,
Wolf das Rauben auch nicht meiden,
Schießt der Jäger, daß es knallt,
Doch, der Wolf ist schon im Wald.

THE WILD PIG.

FROM the green oak wood,
  Where the acorns lie,
Up comes a wild pig,
  Grunting low and high.
Children do not often see
Such a piggy-wig as he!
With his long and slender snout
See him rooting all about,
Poking here, and poking there,
Grubbing up his simple fare,
Roots and nuts and acorns sweet,
Such as piggies love to eat.
Hark! a rustling in the bush!
Off goes piggie with a rush;
Grunting, squealing, there he goes,
Where the forest thickest grows;
And the hunter, brave and gay,
Will not dine on pig to-day!

LAURA E. RICHARDS.

Schwein.

Aus dem grünen Eichenwald,
Wo des Wildes Aufenthalt,
Sieh! kommt auch ein **Schwein** daher,
Läuft die kreuz und läuft die quer,
Sucht sich Nahrung für den Magen:
Eicheln müssen ihm behagen.
Hinter seinen schmalen Backen
Hörst Du sie es wacker knacken.
Jetzt sieht es den Jäger kommen,
Schnell hat es Reißaus genommen.

THE LITTLE WINDOW.

PEEK-A-BOO, light! beautiful light,
Shining so clear through my window bright,
  Down from the sky swiftly you fly—
    Peek-a-boo, beautiful light!

Peek-a-boo, light! beautiful light!
Making the fields and meadows so bright;
  Flowers in the grass smile as you pass—
    Peek-a-boo, beautiful light!

Peek-a-boo, light! beautiful light!
Love is the sunshine that makes the heart bright,
  Pure we would be, shining like thee—
    Peek-a-boo, beautiful light!

EMILY HUNTINGTON MILLER.

THE LITTLE WINDOW.

IN the water, pure and clear,
  Light loves to play;
In the dewdrop's glittering sphere
  Shines the captured ray;
But the firm and solid wall
Gives no gleam of light at all.

Das Fensterlein.

Kind, schau' mein klares Fensterlein,
Dadurch scheint 's Licht in 's Stübchen klein.
Soll Dich stets freun
Des Lichtes Schein,
Mußt Du auch sein
Recht lieb und rein.

Through the parting clouds on high
Streams the sunlight there!
Look! for in the brightening sky
Shines the rainbow fair!
Light can turn the storm-cloud gray
All to gold and crimson gay.

Light is pure and good and fair,
And it loves to rest
Ever on the things that are
Brightest, ay, and best.
Then with smiling faces bright
Let us greet the loving light!

LAURA E. RICHARDS.

THE WINDOW.

"COME, lovely light, and shine on us,
And make us warm and bright.
You shine on us; we'll gaze on you,
For day has conquered night.
In thankful praise of your bright rays,
We lift our happy voices;
For you love us, and we love you,
And all the world rejoices."

"Dear child, the sun has sent me down
To make another day,
And help you tread the path of right
By brightening your way.
In thankful praise of his bright rays,
Then, lift your happy voices;
For you love him, and he loves you,
And all the world rejoices."

GEORGE HYDE PAGE.

Das Fenster.
Sieh, durch 's helle Fensterlein,
Kindchen! kommt das Licht herein;
Sagt: „Möcht' gern beim Kinde sein,
Möcht' dasselbe gern erfreun."
„„Guckguck, Guckguck! du liebes Licht,
Schau freundlich mir in 's Angesicht.""
„Kindchen! bin gelaufen schnell,
Komm' schon von der Sonne hell;
Hab' den Weg gar bald vollbracht,
Weil ich an mein Kind gedacht;
Kindchen liebt ja helles Licht,
Weich' davon, mein Kindchen, nicht."

THE CHARCOAL BURNER.

WHY does the charcoal burner stay
Up in the forest by night and day ?
He chops the trees, and he piles the wood,
And burns it slow to the charcoal good.

The blacksmith's hammer goes "*Kling ! klang ! kling !*
Charcoal ! charcoal hurry and bring !
For how can I shoe the pony's feet,
Without good charcoal the iron to heat ?"

The charcoal burner is black and grim,
But thanks for his labour we owe to him ;
He chops the trees with a whack ! whack ! whack !
And burns the wood to the charcoal black.

Knives and hatchets, shovels and rakes,
Shoes for the pony, the blacksmith makes.
The bellows blow and the hammers beat,
But he must have charcoal the iron to heat.

EMILY HUNTINGTON MILLER.

Die Köhlerhütte.

Klein ist die Köhlerhütte, kaum
Nur für zwei Menschen hat sie
Raum;
Doch wohnen d'rinnen wohlgemuth,
Der Köhler mit seinen Söhnen
gut.
Sie holen das Holz, sie brennen's
zu Kohlen;
Und diese die Schmiede auf Wagen
abholen.
Wie könnte man Messer, Gabeln, Löffel sonst machen
Und noch die nützlichen anderen
Sachen,
Wenn—brennte, mit Kohle und
Ruß im Gesicht,
Der Köhler mit Sorgfalt die
Kohlen uns nicht.

THE CARPENTER.

Busy is the carpenter;
  At his work he stands.
Oh, the wonders he can do
  With his skilful hands!
Sawing now, the long, long boards
  Shorter soon he makes;
And the rough is quickly smoothed
  When the plane he takes.

By his work the crooked soon
  Straight and even grows;
Curved he changes into flat;
  Wondrous skill he shows!
Thus he works so busily,
  But we hear him say
"Here a board, and there a board,
  Pray, what use are they?"

So the carpenter at last
  All together brings,
Nails the boards and timbers fast—
  How his hammer rings!
Thus a cosy house he builds
  Where the child may live;
And for this the grateful child
  Love and thanks will give.

Emilie Poulsson.

Der Zimmermann.

Seht mir nur den Zimmermann,
Welch' seltne Kunst er üben kann:
Was steht bringt er zum Sturz;
Was lang ist, macht er kurz;
Das Runde macht er grad;
Das Rauhe macht er glatt;
Was krumm ist, macht er gleich;
So ist an Kunst er reich.
Das Einzle nicht ihm g'nügt,
Zum Ganzen schnell er's fügt;
Doch, was kommt da heraus?—
Aus Balken wird ein Haus!
Ein Haus für 's gute Kind,
Daß es d'rin Eltern find',
Die sorgsam es bewahren
Vor Seel'- und Leib'sgefahren.
Den Zimmermann das Kind d'rum liebt,
Der ihm den Schutz des Hauses giebt.

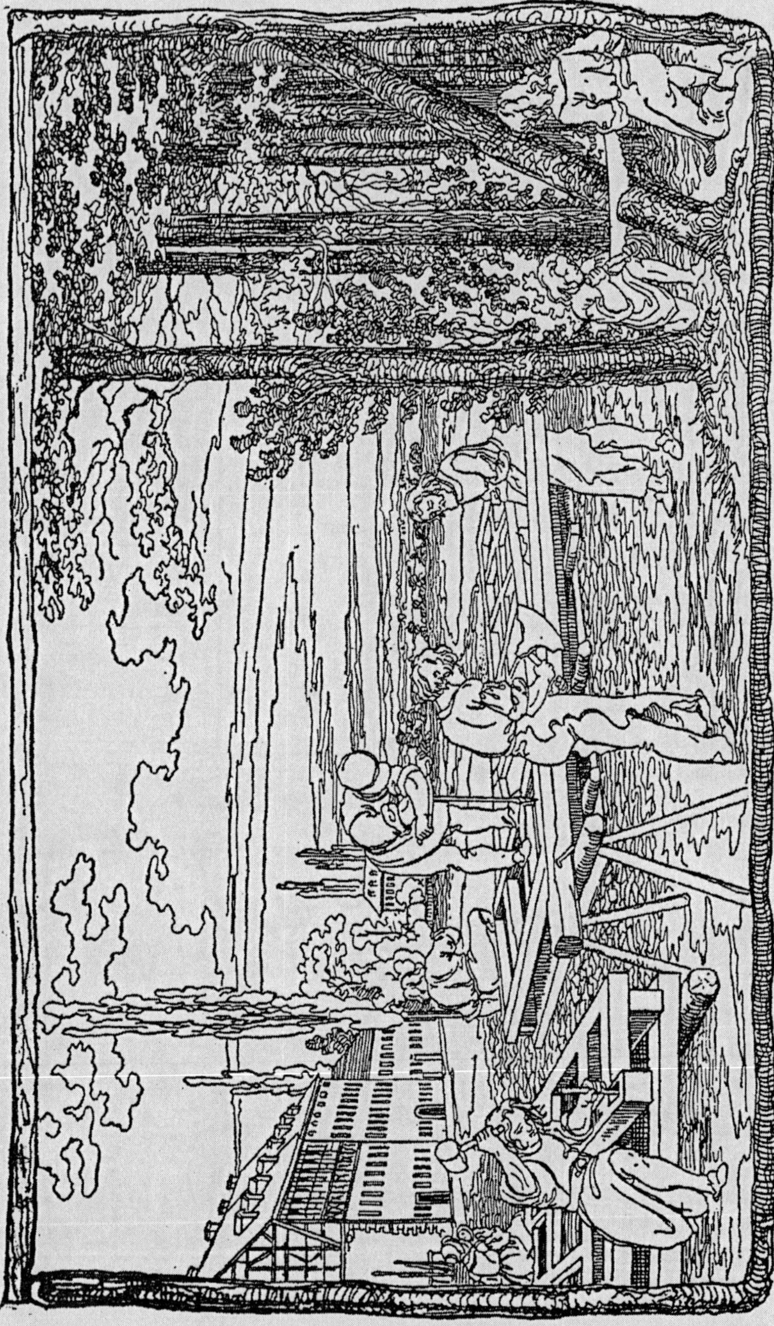

THE BRIDGE.

THE brook is flowing merrily;
  Its waters swiftly glide;
A little child looks longingly
  Beyond its rippling tide.

Across the brook are pretty ferns,
  And oh, such lovely moss!
And flow'rs that seem to nod at him
  And beckon him across.

But dark the water flows between;
  The stream is deep and wide;
No way the little child can find
  To reach the other side.

But soon there comes a carpenter,
  Who works with busy hands,
And builds a bridge that safe and strong
  Above the water stands.

"Oh, thanks to you, good carpenter!"
  The child calls out in glee;
"Now I can reach the other side
  Where I have longed to be."

Then on the bridge the happy child
  Runs back and forth at will,
Although beneath, so deep and wide,
  The brook is flowing still.

EMILIE POULSSON.

Der Steg.

Ein Bächlein fließt das Thal entlang,
'S Kind möcht' hinüber, es wird ihm bang.
Es möchte sich drüben die Blümchen besehn
Und kann doch nicht über das Wasser hingehn.
Zum Gehen führt über das Wasser kein Weg.
Da kommt gleich der Zimmermann, bauet den Steg.
Von hüben nach drüben 's Kind gehen nun kann,
Hab' Dank! Du geschickter Zimmer-
mann.

THE BRIDGE.

WHERE the stream flows swift and fair,
  How shall I cross over ?
In the golden meadows there
  Gaily nods the clover.
"Bring the beam, and bring the plank!
Build a bridge from bank to bank!"

To my friends and playmates dear
  How shall I be showing
All the love that daily here
  In my heart is growing ?
"You must play the joiner's part—
Build a bridge from heart to heart!"

Every loving word you say
  Makes the bridge the stronger;
Helpful deeds from day to day
  Make it last the longer.
Love and joy will banish strife!
So the bridge shall last your life!

LAURA E. RICHARDS.

THE FARMYARD GATE.

JOHNNY, shut the farmyard gate!
Quick, or you will be too late!
Don't you hear the pony neigh?—
"Let us have some fun to-day!
Woods and waters I can see:
Come and try a race with me!"

Pretty cow says: "Moo-oo-oo!
Wait for me; I'm coming too.
I should like to eat my fill
In the pasture bright and still
I should like to stand and drink
At the little brook's green brink."

"Baa!" the sheep say, "let us go
Where the milk-white daisies grow
On the hillsides, warm and steep;
We can nibble grass, or sleep.
Come, old Rover, lead the way—
You will keep us safe to-day."

Lazy pig, with sleepy eyes,
On the straw contented lies;
Chickens peep and pigeons coo;
Loud the cock is crowing too;
Ducks in glossy feathers dressed,
Quack and chatter with the rest.

Hurry, Johnny—do not wait!
Quickly shut the farmyard gate!
Cow, and sheep, and pony dear,
We must keep you safely here!
Bird and bee, you need not stay:
You have wings to fly away.

EMILY HUNTINGTON MILLER.

Das Hofthor.

Was soll dieß sein?— Ein Thor
soll 's sein,
Uns führend in den Hof hinein:
Da springen die Rößlein,
Da fliegen die Täublein,
Da schnattern die Gänschen,
Da quaken die Entchen,
Da pipen die Hühnchen,
Da krähet der Hahn,
Es summen die Bienchen,
Da muhet die Kuh,
Da hüpfet das Kälbchen,
Da mähet das Lämmchen,
Da blöket das Schaf,
Da grunzet das Schwein;
Das Thor muß fest verschlossen sein,
Daß nichts läuft fort,
Ein jedes bleibt an seinem Ort.

THE FARMYARD GATE.

Oh, what a clatter!
Now what's the matter?
The sheep they hurry,
The chickens scurry,
The calf is bawling,
The farmer calling,
"Johnny, run, and shut the gate!"

The cock is crowing,
The cows are lowing,
The ducks are quarking,
The dogs are barking,
The ass is braying,
The horse is neighing:
Johnny! run, and shut the gate!"

The birds are singing,
The bell is ringing,
The pigs are squeaking,
The barn door creaking,
The brook is babbling,
The geese are gabbling:
"Johnny! run, and shut the gate!"

MRS. FOLLEN (adapted by Emily Huntington Miller).

THE GARDEN GATE.

PRETTY garden gate, we pray you
  Open wide, and let us go
Where the merry fountain dances,
  Where the sweet white lilies grow.
    Open, pretty gate, we pray!
    Open, flowers, for now 'tis day!

In the wind so gently rocking,
  Here the mother rose is seen;
And her baby buds are peeping
  Through their blankets soft and green.
    Baby buds, make haste to grow
    While the summer breezes blow!

Darling violets, are you hiding
  In the grass your eyes so blue?
Never fear that we shall harm you—
  We will only smile on you.
    Roses red and lilies white,
    Violets sweet, good-by! good-night!

EMILY HUNTINGTON MILLER.

Das Gartenthor.
„Was soll das sein?—
Ein Thor in den Garten,
Worinne die Gärtner
Die Blümelein warten,
Von mancherlei Arten:
Die duft'gen und zarten,
Oft sanfte behaarten,
In Knöspchen verwahrten,
Auch paarweis gepaarten,
Gleich Schäfchen geschaarten.
Das Thor muß wohl verschlossen sein,
Daß nichts mir stört die Blümchen fein."

THE LITTLE GARDENER.

COME, children, with me to the garden away;
The plants are all waiting our coming to-day;
In heat and in sunshine is drooping each leaf,
But the children are coming to bring them relief.
Trinkle trink! trinkle trink!
How the drops shine and wink,
As the poor thirsty plants hold their heads up to drink!

"All thanks, little children!" each bud seems to say;
"All thanks for the love that you show us to-day!
Now beauty and perfume shall bless you each one,
In loving return for the good you have done.
Twinkle twink! twinkle twink!
Now like stars see us wink!
For kindness brings kindness, so flowers all think."

LAURA E. RICHARDS.

Der kleine Gärtner.

Komm, wir wollen in den Garten,
All' die Pflänzchen dort zu warten:
Wollen sie gar schön begießen.
Das die Knöspchen sich entschließen.
Die Knöspchen sich entfalten nun;
Sie grüßen Dich mit süßem Duft,
Womit sie durchwürzen die ganze
Luft.
Belohnend ist es, wohlzuthun!

THE WHEELWRIGHT.

MARCH together and never stop!
Here we go to the wheelwright's shop!
Wheelwright, show us the way you do,
Making the wheel so round and true.
Turning fast and turning slow,
This is the way the wheel must go!

This is the auger, slim and long,
Turned by the wheelwright's hands so strong.
Straight and steady the auger goes,
And smooth and true the hole it grows.
Turning steady and turning slow,
This is the way the auger must go!

These are the spokes, all shaped aright;
This is the hub that holds them tight;
This is the rim of iron and wood
To finish my wheel so useful and good.
Turning fast and turning slow,
This is the way the wheel must go!

EMILY HUNTINGTON MILLER.

Der Wagner.

Kind, wir woll'n zum Wagner gehn,
Was er macht, genau besehn:
Sieh nur, sieh nur, sieh!
Viel giebt er sich Müh',
Daß der Bohrer grade geh'
Und ein schönes Loch entsteh'.—
Was er wollt', ist fertig nun,
Kann das Rad zur Berre thun:
Die gehet nun immer: rund um,
Rund um, rund um, rund um!

FU.

Der Tischler.

Zisch, zisch, zisch!
Der Tischler hobelt den Tisch.
Tischler, hoble den Tisch mir glatt,
Daß er keine Löcher hat:
Zisch, zisch, zisch!
Tischler, hoble den Tisch.
Lang, lang, lang!
Tischler, hoble die Bank;
Tischler, hoble sie recht blank,
Daß daran kein Span mehr hang';
Lang, lang, lang!
Tischler, hoble die Bank.

THE JOINER.

Plane, plane, plane—
Joiner, follow the grain!
Smooth as silk the table grows;
Not a break the fibre shows.
Plane, plane, plane—
Joiner, follow the grain!

Strong, strong, strong,
Push the plane along!
Make the bench all glossy white;
Not a splinter leave in sight.
Strong, strong, strong,
Push the plane along!

NORA ARCHIBALD SMITH.

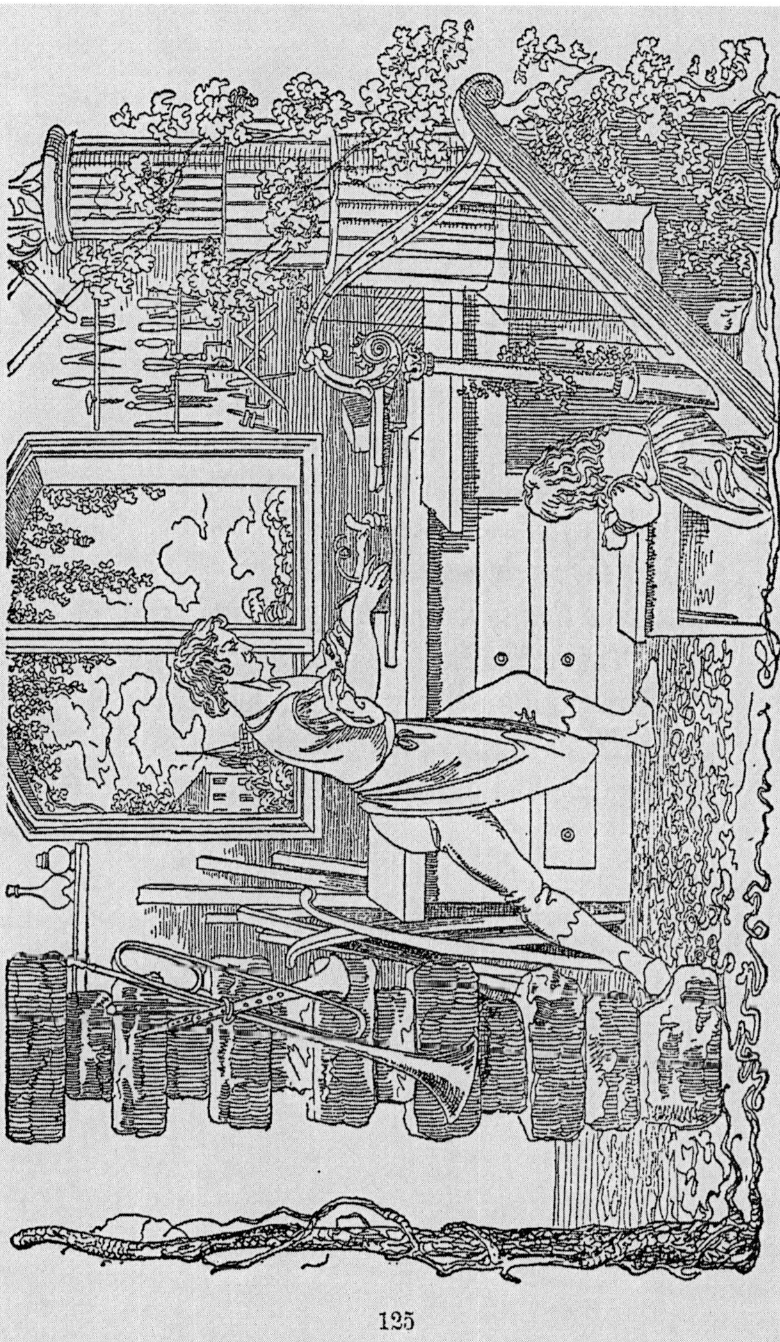

THE KNIGHTS AND THE GOOD CHILD.

GALLOPING fast and galloping free,
Who comes a-riding so swift to me?
"Five brave knights with their plumes so gay.
What do you seek, good knights, to-day?"
"*Over the world we ride to find*
The child that is loving and good and kind."
    "This is the child so dear!
    Brave knights, you see him here!"
"*O child, be always good and gay.*
Now gallop and gallop and gallop away."

EMILY HUNTINGTON MILLER.

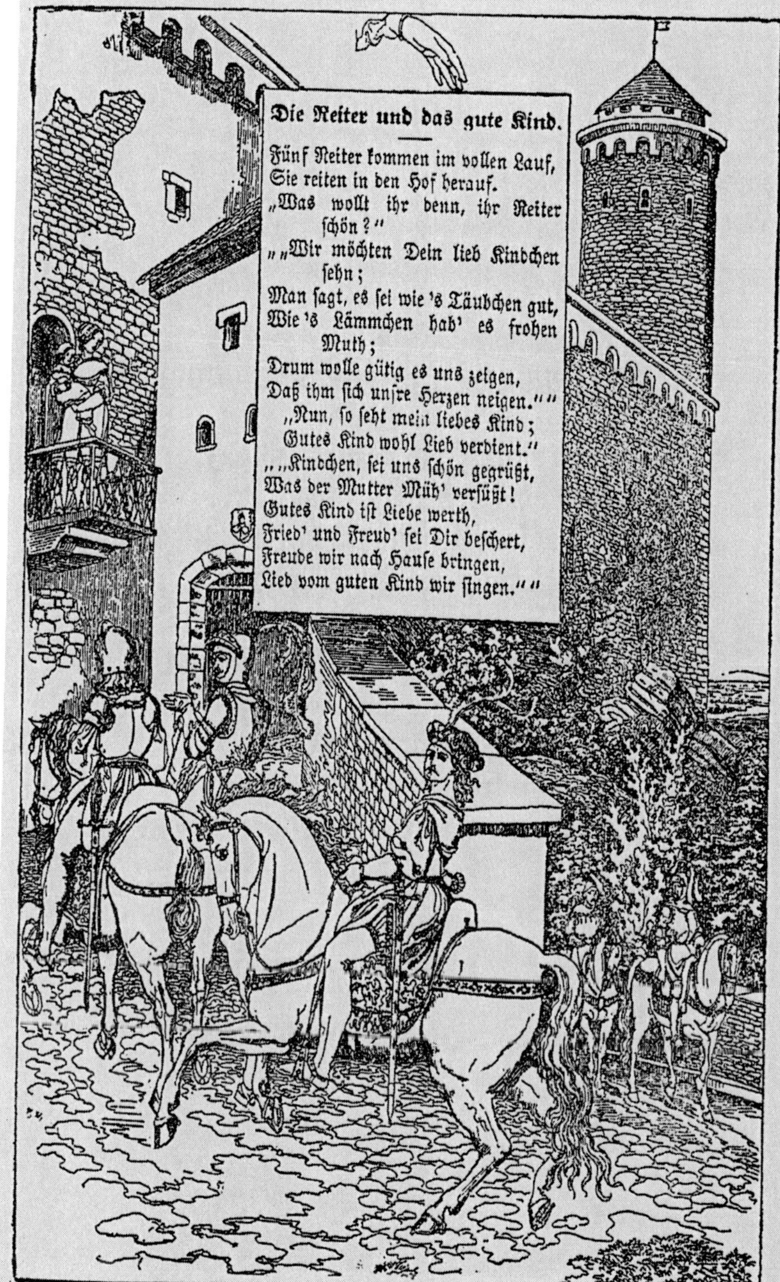
Die Reiter und das gute Kind.
Fünf Reiter kommen im vollen Lauf,
Sie reiten in den Hof herauf.
„Was wollt ihr denn, ihr Reiter schön?“
„„Wir möchten Dein lieb Kindchen sehn;
Man sagt, es sei wie 's Täubchen gut,
Wie 's Lämmchen hab' es frohen Muth;
Drum wolle gütig es uns zeigen,
Daß ihm sich unsre Herzen neigen.““
„Nun, so seht mein liebes Kind;
Gutes Kind wohl Lieb verdient.“
„„Kindchen, sei uns schön gegrüßt,
Was der Mutter Müh' versüßt!
Gutes Kind ist Liebe werth,
Fried' und Freud' sei Dir beschert,
Freude wir nach Hause bringen,
Lied vom guten Kind wir singen.““

THE KNIGHTS AND THE BAD CHILD.

HERE come riding the knights so gay.
"Any good children here," they say,
"Ready to ride with trumpet in hand,
To visit the happy children's land?"
"Ah, brave knights, you will all be sad
To know that my child is selfish and bad."
"It grieves us much to say
He cannot ride to-day.
Only good children with us can go."
Then away and away the knights ride slow.

EMILY HUNTINGTON MILLER

Die Reiter und das mißgelaunte Kind.
Es reiten die Reiter im vollen Lauf,
Sie reiten in den Hof herauf.
„Was wollt ihr denn, ihr Reiter schön?"
„„Wir möchten gern Dein Kindchen sehn!""
„Ach, liebe Reiter, es schreit gar sehr,
Ich bring's nicht zu Euch Reitern her;
Es ist so mürrisch, es ist so kraus,
Es macht uns bald zu eng das Haus."—
„„O, dieß thut uns ja gar zu Leid,
Mit schönen Liebchen wir's gern erfreut;
Doch jetzt wir reiten fort im Lauf
Und suchen uns frömmere Kinder auf.""

THE KNIGHTS AND THE MOTHER.

JINGLE! jingle! jingle!
  Hop! hop! hop!
See, the knights are passing—
  Stop! oh, stop!
Now my child is happy,
  Gentle, good, and true;
He can go a-riding,
  A-riding with you.
A-riding, a-riding, over hill and dell,
But bring him back at evening, because we love him well.

Never fear, my darling.
  Look, and see,
All the knights are smiling,
  Smiling at me.
You shall stay with mother
  Till you older grow;
Then my bonny soldier
  A-riding shall go.
A-riding, a-riding, over hill and dell,
But you'll come back at evening, because we love you well.

EMILY HUNTINGTON MILLER.

Kindchen, verstecke Dich!

Fünf Reiter kommen im vollen Traben,
Sie woll'n so gern mein Kindchen haben.
„Du, mein Kindchen, verstecke Dich,
Daß die Reiter nicht finden Dich."
„Reiter, liebe Reiter,
Reitet immer weiter;
Will 's Euch kurz verkünden,
Könnt mein Kind nicht finden."
Hopp, hopp; hopp, hopp; hopp, hopp;
So reiten sie fort im Galopp.
„Kindchen, schau nun fröhlich auf,
Die Reiter reiten davon im Lauf."

THE KNIGHTS AND THE MOTHER.

I HEAR the bugle sounding
  So merry and so clear;
The knights come gaily riding—
  They want thee, child, I fear.
Now hide thee quick, my darling,
  And nestle close to me,
For not one dimpled finger
  The gallant knights shall see!

You can not have my darling,
  So do not linger here;
Safe in my heart I'll keep him,
  He is so good and dear.
Now do not tarry longer,
  But swiftly ride away!
Peep out and smile, my laddie,
  And bid the knights *Good-day!*

EMILY HUNTINGTON MILLER.

HIDE AND SEEK.

WHERE are you, my baby?
  You've left me alone.
Who'll tell me, who'll tell me
  Where baby is gone?

I've missed him so long;
  He's far, far away,
I'll thank any one
  Who will bring him to stay.

Why, here in my arms
  My dear baby lies!
We often look far
  For what's under our eyes.

HENRIETTA R. ELIOT.

Verstecken des Kindes.

Kindchen, lieb Kindchen Du,
Sag mir, wo weilest Du?—
  Wer sagt, wo mein Kindchen ist?—
  Ich hab' so lang es schon vermißt;
  Ich find' es nicht am alten Ort:
  Fort ist er, fort; fort fort, fort fort.
Wer mir kann mein Kindchen zeigen,
Schönsten Dank will ich ihm reichen.
  Da ist's nun da, das Kindchen ja;
  War dem Herzen ja so nah!—
  „So kann's im Leben oft geschehn,
  Daß man das Nächste nicht kann sehn."

THE CUCKOO!

CUCKOO! cuckoo!
The cuckoo calls you, dear.
Cuckoo! cuckoo!
Call back, and he will hear.
Cuckoo! cuckoo!
The cuckoo is alone.
Cuckoo! cuckoo!
He wants my little one.

HENRIETTA R. ELIOT.

Guckguck!

„Guckguck! Guckguck!“
Der Kuckuck ruft das Kindchen;
„Guckguck! Guckguck!“
Ruf' ihn doch auch geschwindchen;
„Guckguck! Guckguck!“
Der Kuckuck ist so ganz allein,
„Guckguck! Guckguck!
Er möchte gern beim Kindchen sein,
„Guckguck! Guckguck!“
Jetzt hat ihn gefunden mein Kindchen klein,
Nun können sie fröhlich beisammen sein.

THE TOYMAN AND THE MAIDEN.

LISTEN! listen, mother dear,
  How the bells are ringing!
"*Christmas times will soon be here,*"
  That is what they're singing.

All the boys and girls are out
  In the frosty weather;
I can hear them laugh and shout,
  As they talk together.

All the shops with toys are gay,
  Such a pretty showing;
Mother, dear, this very day
  Let us too be going.

Don't you think if Santa Claus
  Down this way were straying,
He would stop and smile to hear
  What the folks were saying?

I am sure if he should see
  Just what I was choosing,
Such a wise old dear as he
  Would not be refusing.

Mother, dear, your little maid
  Will not fret or tease you;
All the year I've surely tried
  To be good and please you.

But if I should give your hand
  Just a little squeezing
When the loveliest doll I see,
  Would you call that teasing?

EMILY HUNTINGTON MILLER.

„„Schau, gar nette Spinnerädchen,
Eine Küche, Küchengeräth,
Teller, Schüsseln, Töpfebrett;
Alles ist blink-blank, ist niedlich und fein
Wie ein recht sorgliches Töchterlein.““
„Wenn, Kaufmann, nun das Christkind-
chen kommt,
Sag' ihm, Amalie sei hier gewesen;
Es möchte für sie was Schönes auslesen,
Was sie erfreue, und was auch ihr frommt;
Sie sei ein gutes, ein williges Kind,
Es folge auf Winke und Worte geschwind.“

Der Kaufmann und der Knabe.

Vater, Vater! sei so gut,
Nimm doch Deinen Stock und Hut;
Laß uns schnell zum Kaufmann gehn,
All' sein Schönes zu besehn:
Schafe, Rinder, Hirt und Heerde,
Und vor allem rasche Pferde;
Vater, Vater! bitte, bitt',
Nimm mich doch zum Kaufmann mit.
Christfestjahrmarkt ist ja heut,
Der so schöne Sachen beut.
„Knabe, kannst wohl mit mir gehen,
All' sein Schönes zu besehen;
Eins doch muß ich Dir vertraun:
Die Sachen den Vater gar finster anschaun,
Wenn ihn ein kleiner Knabe begleitet,
Welcher nicht folgt, das Schlechte nicht meidet;
Welcher nicht immer ist fleißig und gut,
Der nicht hat sinnigen, frohen Muth.
Und wenn dem Vater für 's Kind nichts gefällt,
Das Christkindchen auch für den Knaben nichts wählt."
Vater, mein Vater! o komm nur und komm!
Will schon recht tüchtig sein, wacker und fromm.

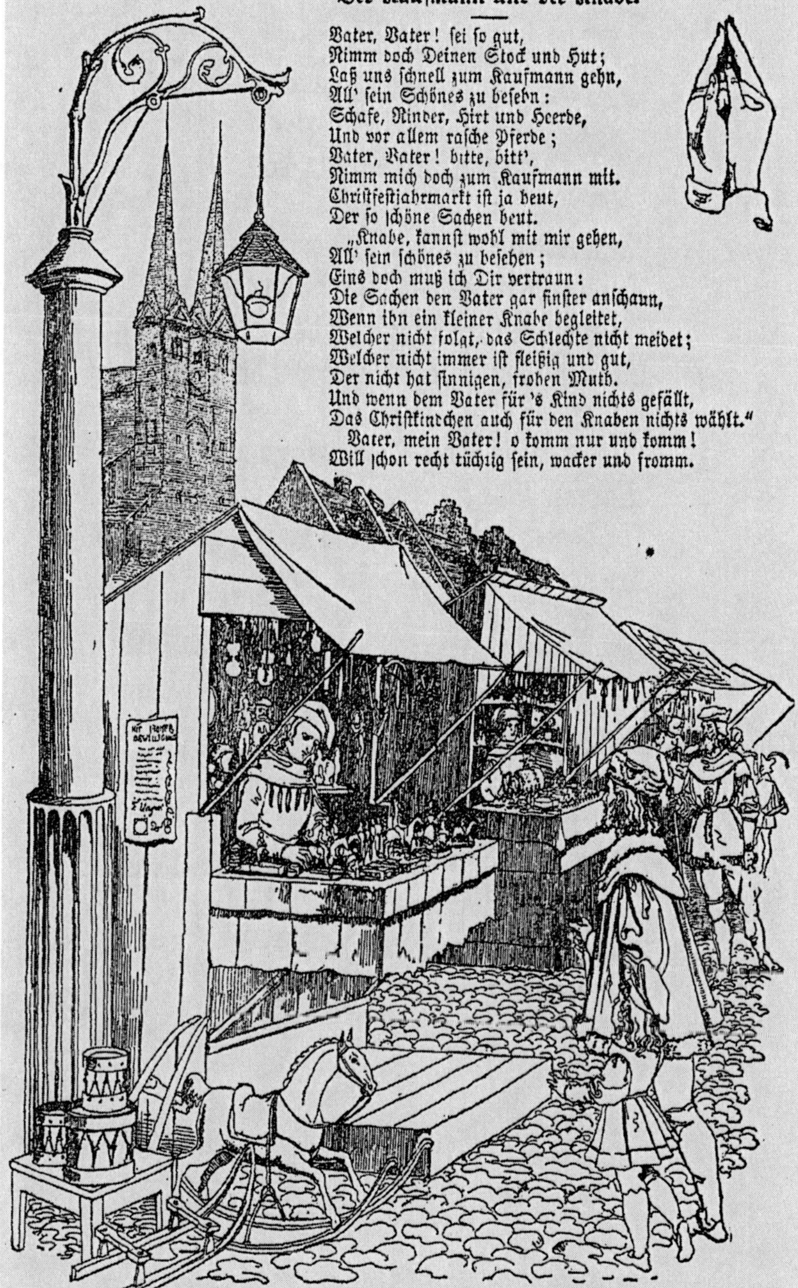

THE TOYMAN AND THE BOY.

"HASTEN, dear father, and come with me
The toyman's wonderful shop to see!
We must tell the toyman what to say,
If Santa Claus happens to come his way."

"But what if Santa Claus asks me, dear,
'*Has this little child been good this year?*'
For books, and puzzles, and games, and toys,
Are not for idle and selfish boys."

"Then tell him, father, that every day
I try to be loving and quick to obey;
And every year, as I older grow,
I shall be wiser and better, I know."

"Now, toyman, what can you show me here
To please a child that is good and dear?"
"Beautiful things I have to sell;
I am too busy their names to tell.

" Here are trumpets to blow, and drums to beat;
Here are knights and soldiers, and horses fleet;
Here are bows and arrows, and sleds to use,
And games and puzzles, and books to choose."

" Toyman, listen! perhaps some day,
Santa Claus may be coming this way;
Here is a message to slip in his hand;
I think good Santa will understand.

" He may bring a drum, and a fine new sled
Swift as an arrow, and painted red;
A pair of skates, and a book that tells
Of knights and fairies and Christmas bells.

" But tell him, toyman, in yonder street
Are poor little children with bare cold feet;
He must bring them stockings, all warm and
new,
And caps and mittens, and playthings too.

" And, toyman, lest he should happen to lack,
Here is some money to fill up his pack;
We send them our greetings, and wish them
good cheer
For a merry Christmas and Happy New Year."

EMILY HUNTINGTON MILLER.

Kirchenthür mit Fenster.

„Wo sich Einklang in der Mehrheit zeiget,
Wo er in Gestalt und Tönen spricht,
Da sich früh des Kindes Sinn hinneiget,
Dieß zu pflegen, Eltern, säumet nicht:
Laßt vor Allem früh das Kindchen ahnen,
Daß ein höchstes Streben alle eint.
Höchstes Lebensglück früh anzubahnen,
Nicht so schwer ist 's, wie Ihr meint.
Doch muß dieser Sinn selbst in Euch leben,
Seele sein, von Allem, was Ihr thut;
Höchstes habt Ihr so dem Kind gegeben,
Schützend nun es in sich selber ruht.—
Nichts ist mehr im Stand, es ihm zu rauben,
Innig eins ist 's im Gemüth und Geist.
Gebt dem Kinde, Eltern! solchen Glauben,
Es Euch durch sein ganzes Leben preist.
Meinet nicht, dazu sei 's noch zu kleine,
Ein Magnet im kleinsten Kinde liegt,
Der ihm zeigt, wo Lebenseinigung eine,
Und auch welcher Sinn durch Trennung trügt."

THE CHURCH.

HARK! the church bell's pleasant sound;
Let us go, my child,
There, where every Sunday morn
Rings the summons mild.
Through the lofty windows there
Rainbow light is streaming fair;
From the doors, wide open thrown,
Peals the organ's solemn tone.
CHORUS—"Come!" says the silver bell,
"Come, where the voices tell
Of the God, that dwells above,
Of the God, whose name is love."

Let your heart be pure and clean
When to church you go,
For all sweet and lovely things
There you'll learn to know.
Learn of God, who gives us all—
Birds that sing and streams that fall,
Sun and moon in glorious might,
Trees and flowers in beauty bright.
CHORUS—"Come!" says the silver bell, etc.

God, who sends the merry breeze
    Blowing here and there,
Sends the mighty storms that rage
    Through the upper air;
Yet so loving kind is he,
Every smallest leaf you see
Knows his care and does his will,
Owns his wisdom, working still.
CHORUS—"Come!" says the silver bell, etc.

In the church, so calm, so still,
    When your childish heart
With a solemn joy doth fill,
    That, too, is his part.
He, who loving parents gave,
Sister sweet and brother brave,
Gives the power to love and bless,
Bringing joy and happiness.
CHORUS—"Come!" says the silver bell, etc.

Once he sent, to dwell on earth,
    Jesus, blessed child,
From the hour that gave him birth
    Pure and undefiled.
Try, like him, my little child,
To be gentle, kind, and mild:
For 'tis thus your love you'll show
To the God who loves you so.
CHORUS—"Come!" says the silver bell, etc.

LAURA E. RICHARDS

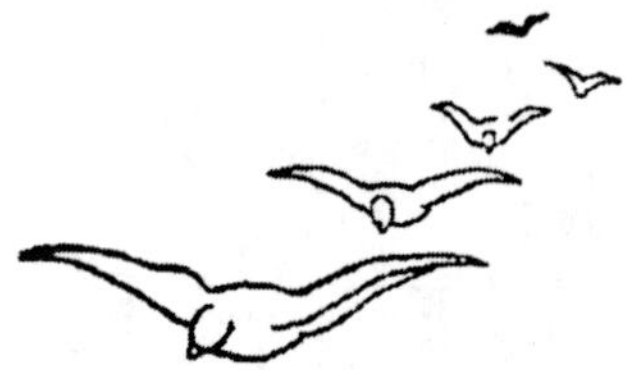

OH, now we'll draw
such pretty things!
See! little birds with
outspread wings,

The sloping hill o'er which
they fly

To reach a tree with branches
high—
The tree these birdies love the
best,

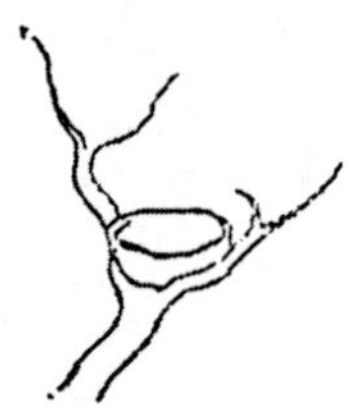

Because it holds their own dear
nest.

That was the birdies' home,
and here
We'll draw the children's home,
so dear;

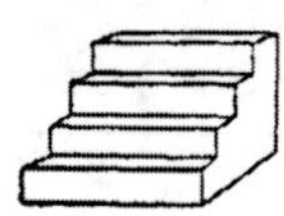

And leading to the very door
Are all these steps—one, two, three,
four.

The window now we'll draw, where we
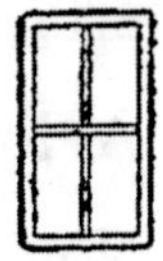
Look out so many things to see.
O window clear and bright, 'tis you
That let the lovely light pass through!
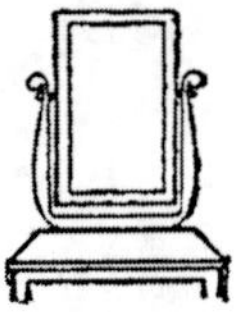
When sunbeams on this mirror fall,
The light-bird dances on the wall.

Now, if you could but look
behind

The house, this rippling brook
you'd find,
Where swim so many silvery
fish:

And if to cross the brook you
wish,
Why, here's the bridge, so
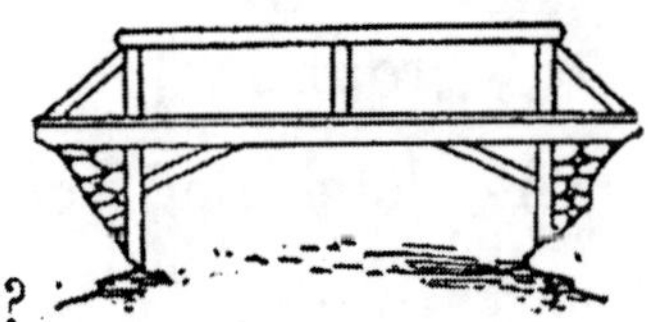
safe and dry.
Shall we go over, you and I?

What's this? A watering can like

ours,
To fill with water for the flowers.

And now we draw a ladder—see!
A long, long ladder it shall be.
No wonder baby thought he soon
With this could reach the shining moon.

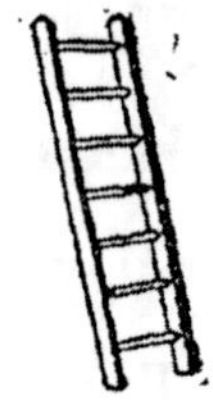

Now here's a cosey pigeon house,
Not hid in any leafy boughs,
But set upon this pole so tall;
Here safely live the pigeons all,

And coo with voices
soft and low
As in and out their
house they go.

Down far below them on the
ground
The hen and chickens walk
around.

And see! a rabbit next
appears;

O bunny, you have such long
ears!

And here's the farmyard gate,
which we
Should always close so carefully.

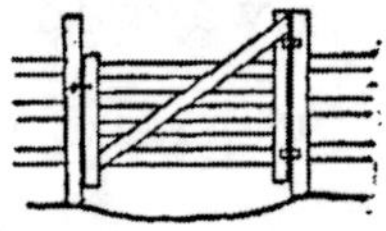

Now, for the carpenter, we'll draw
A hammer—see! and this sharp saw;
And always gratefully we'll tell
About the house he built so well.

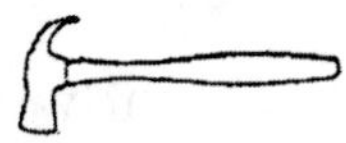

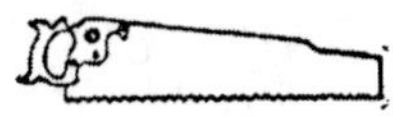

More friends like him we
have, so kind,
We like to bring them to
our mind.

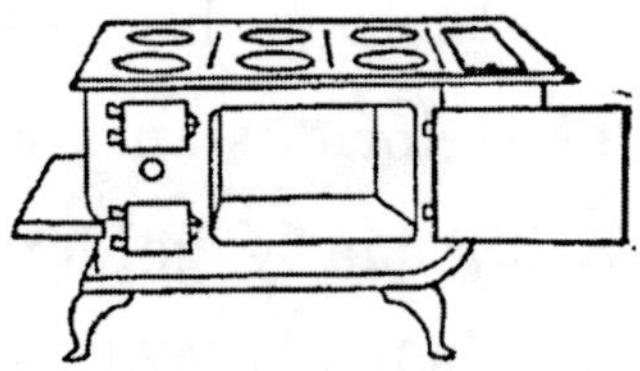

So, baker, since our bread you bake,
An oven now for you we'll make.
And, miller, for the wheat you grind,
This flour barrel you shall find.

Good farmer, here's your harrow
now;
We'll draw, besides, the useful
plough:

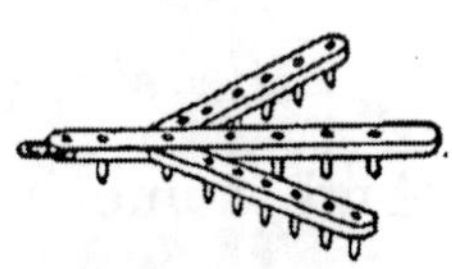

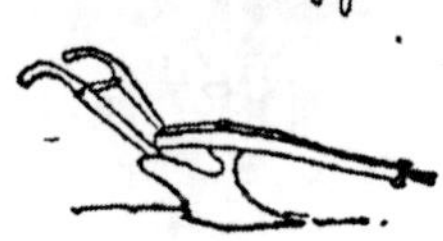

A waggon, too, to load with hay,
Or grain, or fruit, some
harvest day.

And now we draw a wheel alone,
Where hub and tire and spokes are
shown.

But look! Far over in the
sky
A dazzling wheel shines
there on high—

The glorious sun, whose spreading rays
Bring many golden, happy days.
And when night darkens all the blue,
The twinkling stars come peeping
through.

Our eyes the wondrous windows
are
Through which we gaze on sun
and star;

And sometimes what we see on
high,

We find in beauty nearer by;
For star shapes glitter in the snow,
And star flowers, too, the meadows show.

And now we'll draw the moon, whose
  light
Makes beautiful the silent night:

Sometimes a crescent, thin and clear,
Sometimes a big, round, silver sphere;
But whether round, or like a bow,
It is the same dear moon, we know.

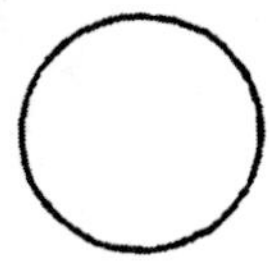

Now we will draw but one thing more,
And that shall be the big church door.
But drawing is such happy play,
We'll surely draw again some day.

EMILIE POULSSON.

SONGS AND GAMES.

PLAY WITH THE LIMBS.

EMILY HUNTINGTON MILLER. OLD ENGLISH (*17th Century*).

PLAY WITH THE LIMBS.

M. J. GARLAND. *Adapted from a Tyrolese Folk Song.*

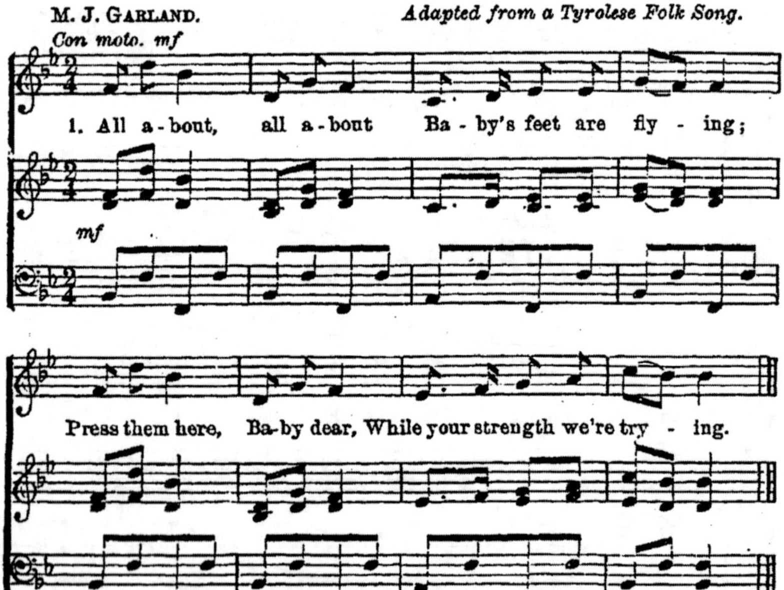

FALLING! FALLING!

EMILIE POULSSON. FRED. FIELD BULLARD, Opus 30, No. 3.

THE WEATHERVANE.

EMILIE POULSSON. GEORGE L. OSGOOD.

Moderato. (Well accented.)

THE WEATHERVANE.

EMILIE POULSSON. *Arranged from* ROBERT KOHL, *by* E. S.

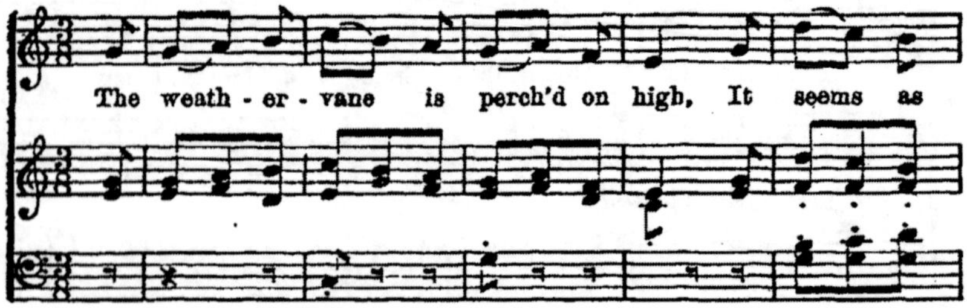

THE TREES.

From "Music for the Kindergarten," by ELEANOR HEERWART.

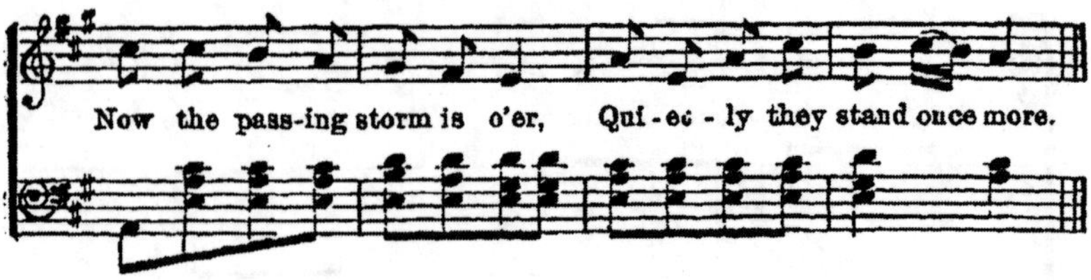

THE WIND MILL.

LOUIS C. ELSON. *Arranged from* ADOLPH JENSEN.

Allegretto.

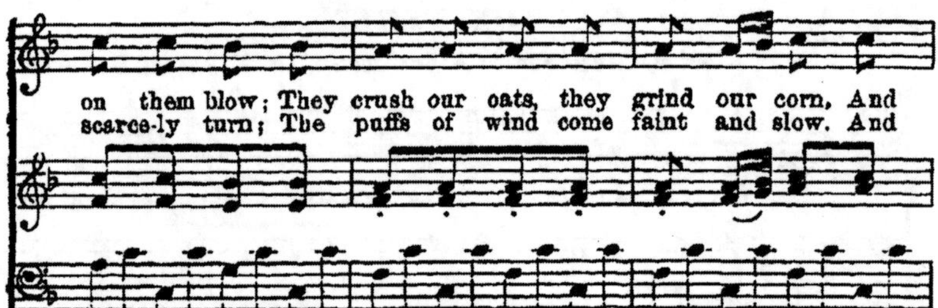

Words from WIDE AWAKE, by permission of D. Lothrop Company.

From "Songs for Little Children," for the Kindergarten and Primary Schools, by Eleanor Smith. Publishers: Milton Bradley Co., Springfield, Mass.; Thos Charles Co., Chicago. With permission of author and publishers.

vem - ber gales, Swift go the arms and full the sails; With
pleas - ure sees How light and light - er, grows the breeze; And
joy the miller's heart doth swell, He knows his mill is grinding well.
soon, a - las! it whol - ly drops, And then the bus - y wind-mill stops.

WIND SONG.

ROBERT LOUIS STEVENSON. E. S.

From "Songs for Little Children," for the Kindergarten and Primary Schools, by Eleanor Smith. Publishers: Milton Bradley Co., Springfield, Mass.; Thos. Charles Co., Chicago. With permission of author and publishers.

ALL GONE.

EMILY HUNTINGTON MILLER. FRED. FIELD BULLARD, Op. 30, No. 8.

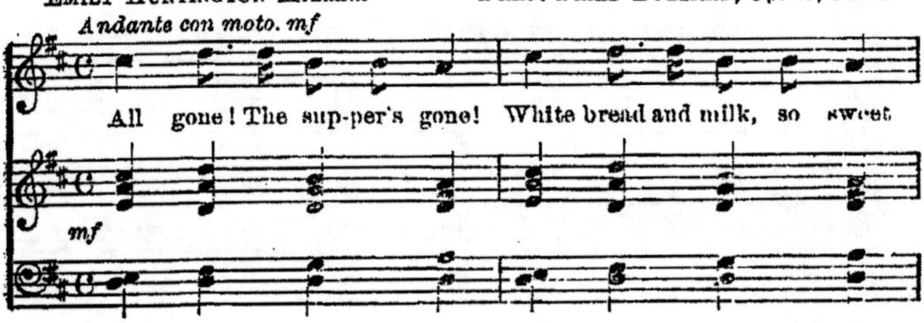

cres - - - - - - - cen - - - - - - do.
Lit - tle mouth with o - pen lips, Thro' your ro - sy gate it slips;
cres - - - - - - - cen - - - - - - do.
mf
Lit - tle throat, you know full well Where it went, if you would tell.
mf
f
Lit - tle hands! grow strong: Lit - tle legs! grow long;
f
Lit - tle cheeks! grow red; You have all been fed.

TASTE.—Guessing Game.

NORA ARCHIBALD SMITH. FRED. FIELD BULLARD, Op. 30, No. 6.

FLOWER SONG.

NORA ARCHIBALD SMITH. *Adapted from an old Scotch Melody.*

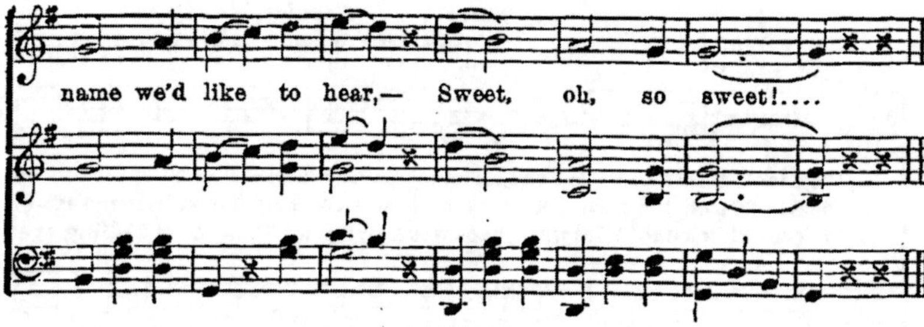

FLOWER SONG.

KATE L. BROWN. CARL REINECKE.

TICK-TACK!

Popular Melody from
"Childrens' Songs," by CARL REINECKE.

EMILIE POULSSON.

TICK! TOCK!

EMILY HUNTINGTON MILLER. ELEANOR SMITH.

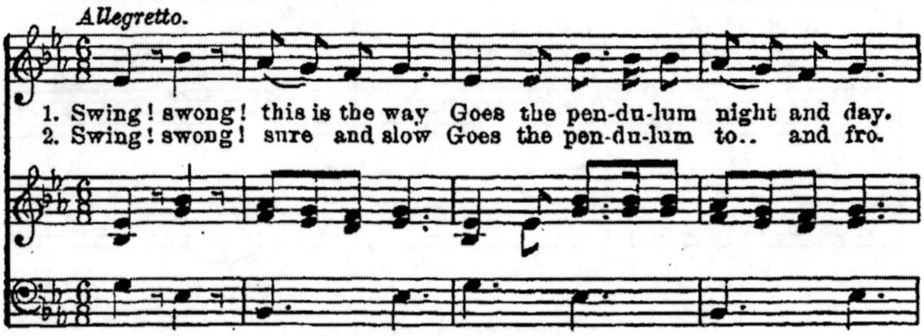

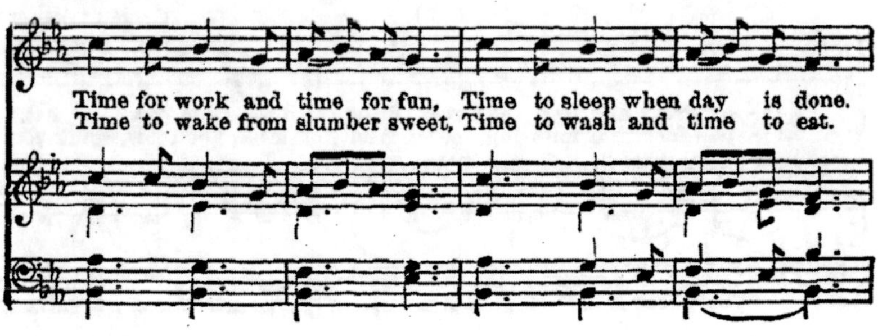

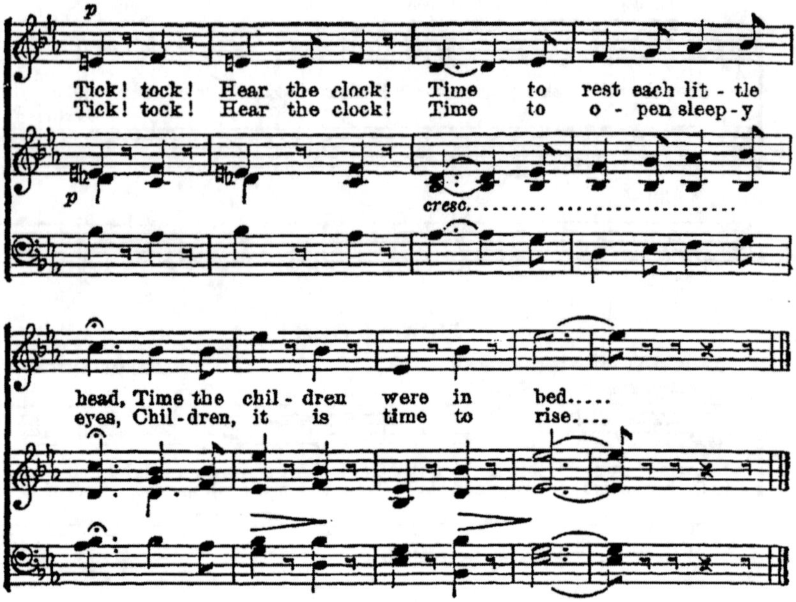

MOWING GRASS.

EMILIE POULSSON. *German Folk Song.*

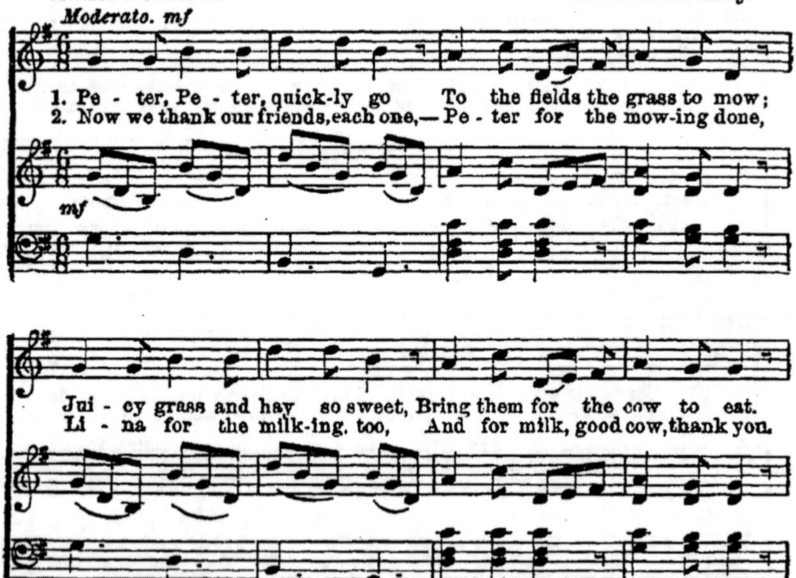

* Pronounced Lee-na.

BECKONING THE CHICKENS.

EMILY HUNTINGTON MILLER. W. W. GILCHRIST.

BECKONING THE PIGEONS.

EMILIE POULSSON. *Arranged from* KARL REINECKE, *by* ELEANOR SMITH.

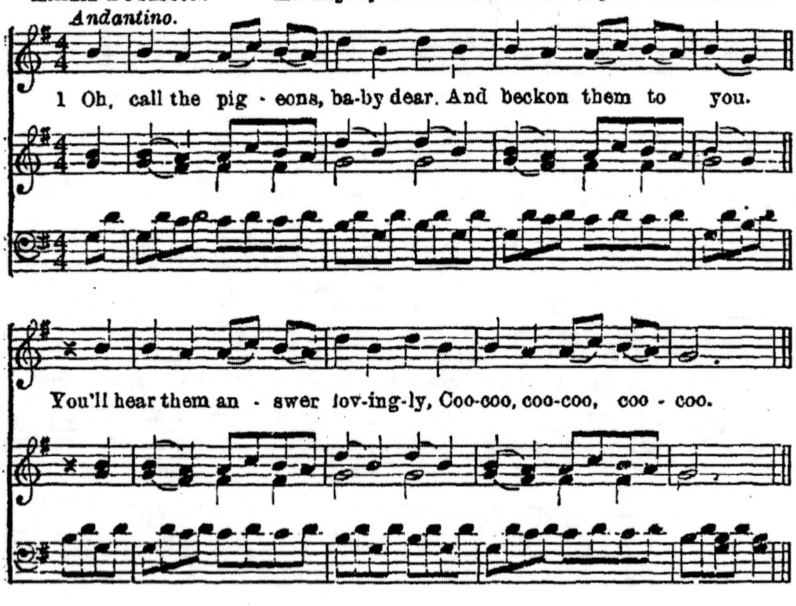

THE FISH IN THE BROOK.

Words adapted from "Music for the Kindergarten," by ELEANOR HEERWART.

Arranged from ROBERT KOHL, *by* E. S.

THE FISH IN THE BROOK.

EMILY HUNTINGTON MILLER.

Music adapted from
JOHANNES BRAHMS, *by* E. S.

THE CATERPILLAR.

EMILIE POULSSON. ELEANOR SMITH.

BUTTERFLIES.

KATE L. BROWN. ELIZABETH U. EMERSON.

From "Stories in Song," told by Elizabeth U. Emerson, and Kate S. Brown. By arrangement with Oliver Ditson Co.

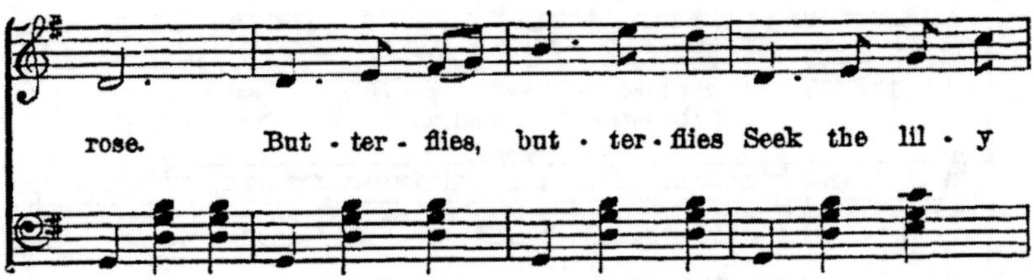

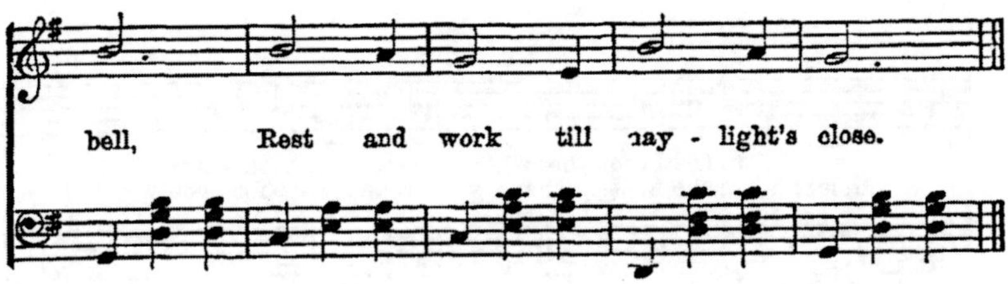

THE FLYING BIRD.

KATE L. BROWN. W. W. GILCHRIST.

Rather fast, but with smooth, undulating motion.

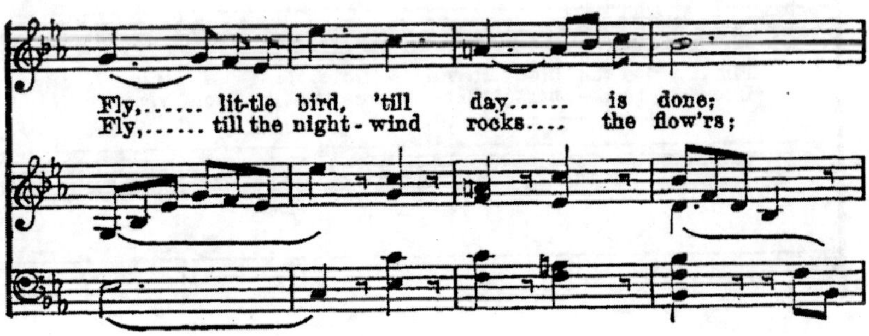

Fly,...... lit-tle bird, where grass - - es play;
Fly....... thro' the twi - light and sil - - - - ver dew,
Fly...... to the blue heav'n far.......... a - way:
Home... to the nest that waits....... for you.
Fly! fly! fly! Fly! fly! fly!
Fly! fly! fly! Fly! fly! fly!
Fly..... to the blue heav'n far...... a - way.
Home... to the nest that waits... for you.

THE TARGET.

EMILY HUNTINGTON MILLER. FRED. FIELD BULLARD, Op. 30, No. 5.

PAT-A-CAKE.

EMILY HUNTINGTON MILLER. *Alsatian Folk Song.*

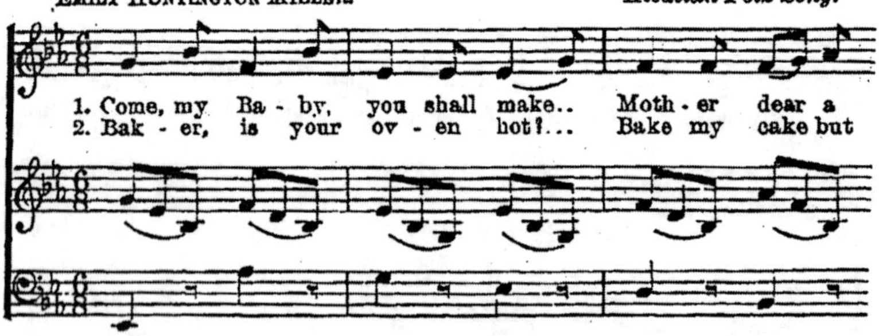

THE MILL-WHEEL.

KATE L. BROWN. CARL REINECKE.

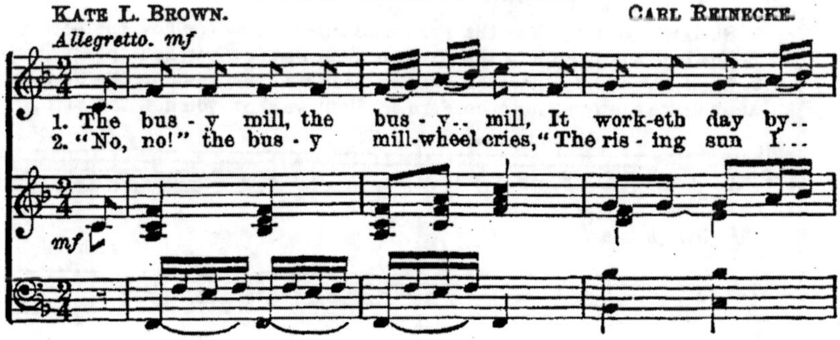

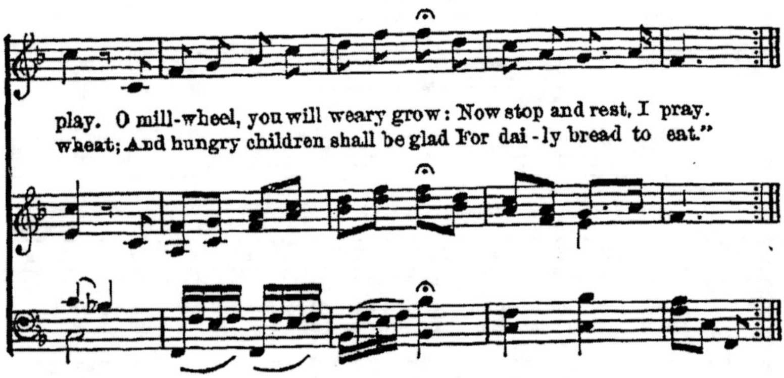

THE FARMER.

Melody adapted from Swiss Folk Song.

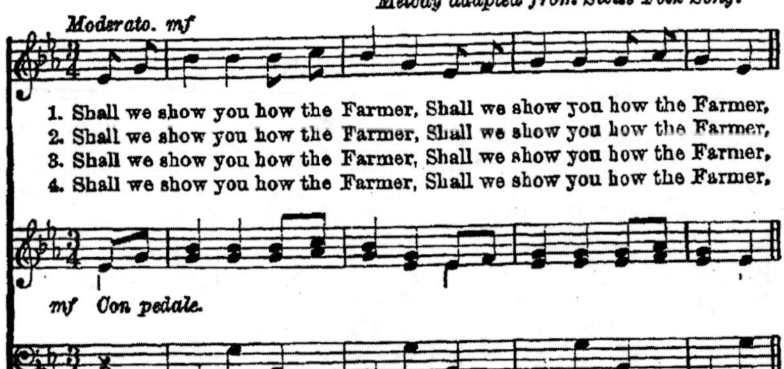

Shall we show you how the Farm-er sows his bar - ley and wheat?
Shall we show you how the Farm-er mows his bar - ley and wheat?
Shall we show you how the Farm-er threshes bar - ley and wheat?
Shall we show you how the Farm-er sifts his bar - ley and wheat?
f
Look, 'tis thus the bus-y Farm-er, Look, 'tis thus the bus-y Farm-er,
Look, 'tis thus the bus-y Farm-er, Look, 'tis thus the bus-y Farm-er,
Look, 'tis thus the bus-y Farm-er, Look, 'tis thus the bus-y Farm-er,
Look, 'tis thus the bus-y Farm-er, Look, 'tis thus the bus-y Farm-er,
f
Look, 'tis thus the bus-y Farm-er sows his bar - ley and wheat.
Look, 'tis thus the bus-y Farm-er mows his bar - ley and wheat.
Look, 'tis thus the bus-y Farm-er thresh-es bar - ley and wheat.
Look, 'tis thus the bus-y Farm-er sifts his bar - ley and wheat.

THE BIRD'S NEST.

KATE L. BROWN. *Arranged from* ROBERT KOHL, *by* E. S.

IN A HEDGE.

FROEBEL. E. S.

From "Songs for Little Children," for the Kindergarten and Primary Schools, by Eleanor Smith. Publishers: Milton Bradley Co., Springfield, Mass.; Thomas Charles Co., 211-213, Wabash Avenue, Chicago. With permission of author and publishers.

THE BIRD'S NEST.

EMILY HUNTINGTON MILLER. W. W. GILCHRIST.

In moderate time, and with an easy swing.

WHAT DOES LITTLE BIRDIE SAY?

TENNYSON. E. S.

LULLABY.

J. W. ELLIOTT.

Andante con moto.

cres.
Qui - et as mice in church-es, He puts his head where no one knows,
cres.
pp
On one leg he perch - es. When lit-tle Ba - by bye-bye goes,
pp legato e ben sostenuto.
poco cres.
cres.
On Mama's arm re - pos - ing; Soon he lies be - neath the clothes, Safe
poco cres.
cres.
rall.
in the cra-dle doz - ing.
colla voce.
mp
cres - - -

p
When pretty Pus - sy
cen - - do. dim. ritard. p
goes to sleep, Tail and nose to - geth - er, Then lit-tle mice a -
round her creep, Light-ly as a feath - er. When lit-tle Ba - by
pp
pp legato e ben sostenuto.
goes to sleep, And he is ver - y near us, Then on tip - toe
pp
pp

BIRD THOUGHTS.

Author Unknown. W. W. GILCHRIST.

THE FLOWER BASKET.

KATE L. BROWN. R. KOHL.

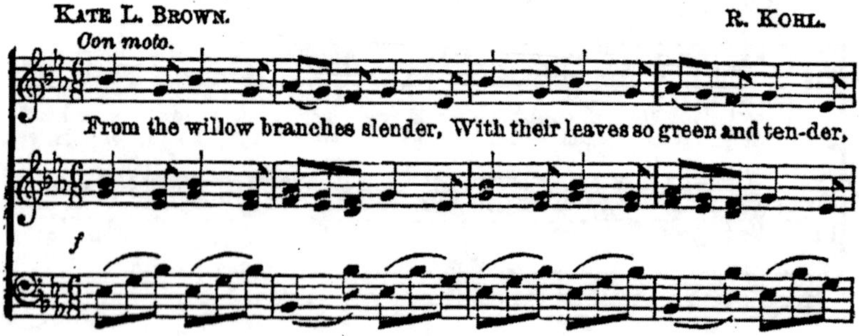

Lit - tle baskets we are weaving, All our sweetest flowers receiv-ing ;
To.. our parents we are bringing Pret-ty gifts with joy and singing:
La, la, la, la, Dearest Pa-pa, Flow'rs we bring to you,......
La, la, la, la, Dearest Mama, Flow'rs we bring to you.......

EMILY HUNTINGTON MILLER. ELEANOR SMITH.

THE PIGEON-HOUSE.

EMILY HUNTINGTON MILLER. ROBERT KOHL, *arr. by* E. S.

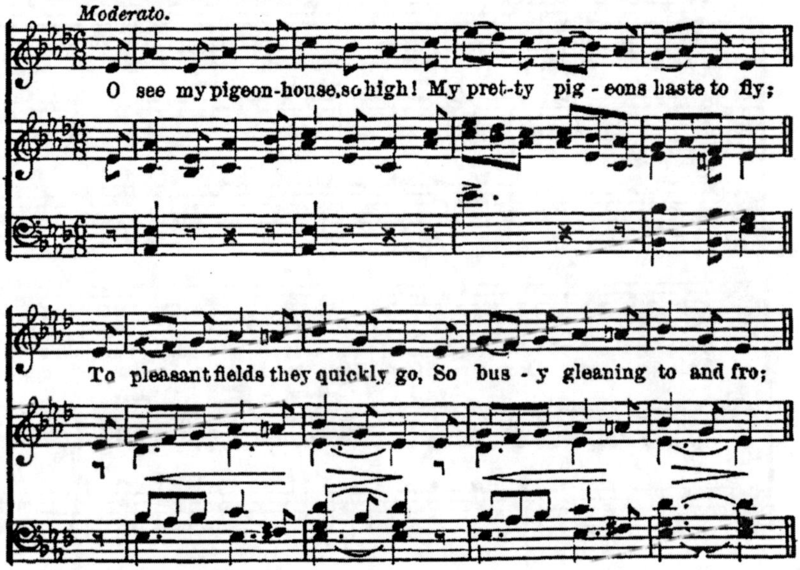

NAMING THE FINGERS.

LAURA E. RICHARDS. *French Folk Song.*

Andante non troppo. mf dolce.

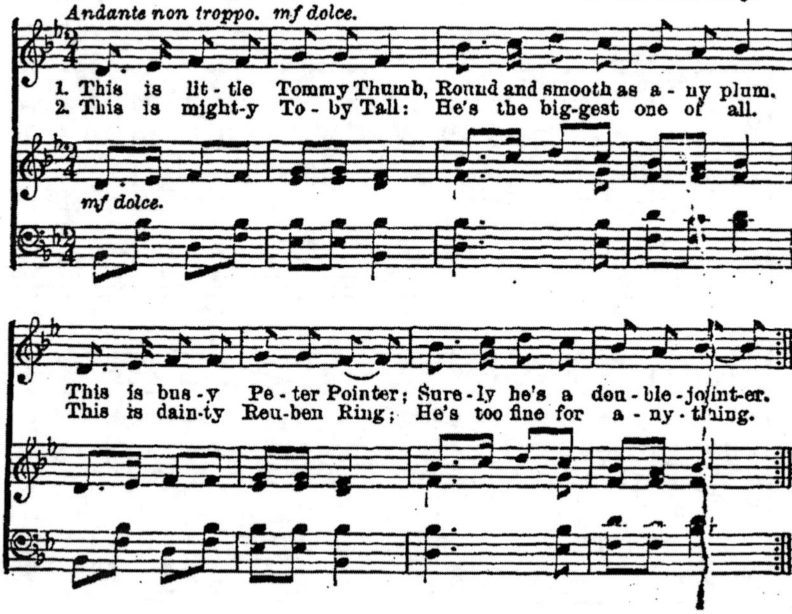

rall.
3. And this lit - tle wee one, may be, Is the pret-ty Fin-ger Ba - by.
rall.
a tempo.
All the five we've counted now, Bus - y Fin-gers in a row.
a tempo.
Ev - 'ry Fin - ger knows the way, How to work and how to play;
lento e marcato.
But to - geth er they work best, Each one help-ing all the rest.
lento e marcato.

THE GREETING.

EMILIE POULSSON. *Adapted from a Scotch Folk Song.*

THUMBS AND FINGERS SAY, "GOOD MORNING."

Words adapted from FROEBEL. E. S.

From "Songs for Little Children," for the Kindergarten and Primary Schools, by Eleanor Smith. Publishers: Milton Bradley Co., Springfield, Mass.; Thos. Charles Co., Chicago. With permission of author and publishers.

THE FAMILY.

EMILIE POULSSON. W. W. GILCHRIST.

THE FAMILY.

EMILIE POULSSON. EUPHEMIA M. PARKER.

Lento ma non troppo. mp dolce. *(The Refrain after a French Folk Song.)*

This is the bus - y Fa - ther, Brave and full of cheer;
This is the mer - ry Broth - er, Grown so strong and tall;....
This is the gen - tle Sis - ter, This the Ba - by small...
And here they all to - geth - er meet, This whole glad fam-i - ly complete.

THE FAMILY.

EMILIE POULSSON. *Austrian Folk Song.*

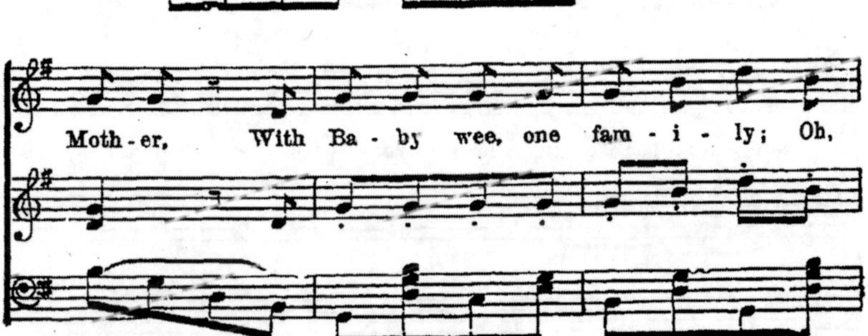

*, for right hand.

† 2, for left hand.

EMILIE POULSSON. *Adapted from a French Folk Song.*

(LULLABY. *Peruvian Slumber Song.*)

GO TO SLEEP, THUMBKIN.

Adapted from FROEBEL. E. S.

FIVE IN A ROW.

Adapted from REINECKE.

From "Songs for Little Children," for the Kindergarten and Primary Schools, by Eleanor Smith. Publishers: Milton Bradley Co., Springfield, Mass.; Thomas Charles Co., 211-213, Wabash Avenue, Chicago. With permission of author and publishers.

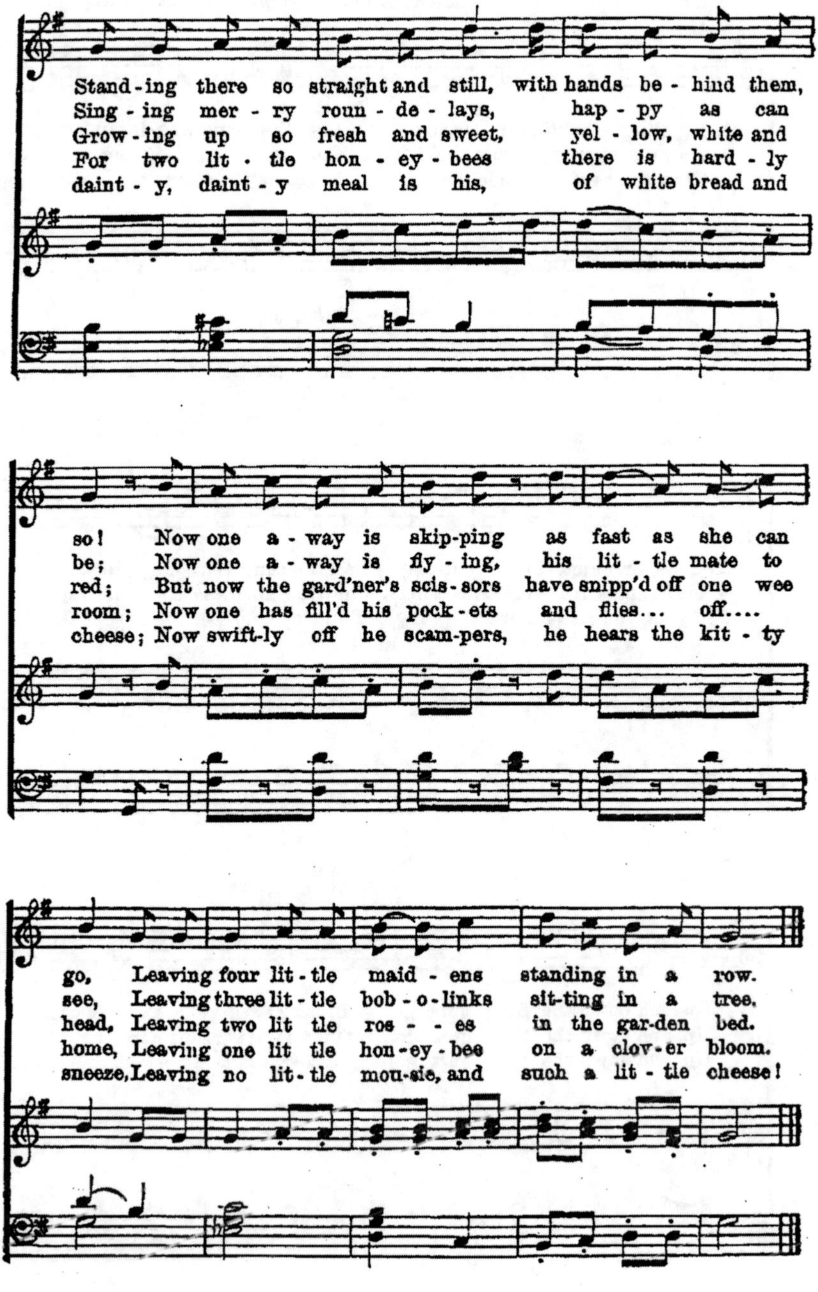
Stand-ing there so straight and still, with hands be-hind them,
Sing-ing mer-ry roun-de-lays, hap-py as can
Grow-ing up so fresh and sweet, yel-low, white and
For two lit-tle hon-ey-bees there is hard-ly
daint-y, daint-y meal is his, of white bread and
so! Now one a-way is skip-ping as fast as she can
be; Now one a-way is fly-ing, his lit-tle mate to
red; But now the gard'ner's scis-sors have snipp'd off one wee
room; Now one has fill'd his pock-ets and flies... off....
cheese; Now swift-ly off he scam-pers, he hears the kit-ty
go, Leaving four lit-tle maid-ens standing in a row.
see, Leaving three lit-tle bob-o-links sit-ting in a tree.
head, Leaving two lit tle ros-es in the gar-den bed.
home, Leaving one lit tle hon-ey-bee on a clov-er bloom.
sneeze, Leaving no lit-tle mou-sie, and such a lit-tle cheese!

FINGER PIANO.

KATE L. BROWN. *Music arranged from* CARL REINECKE, *by* E. S.

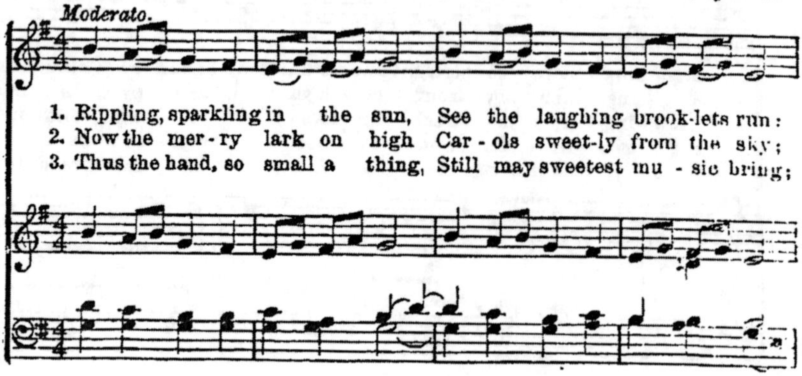

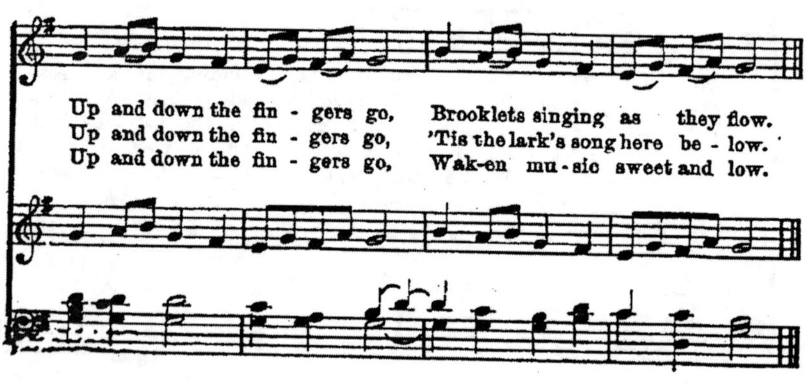

LAURA E. RICHARDS. *Old French Lullaby.*

THE BABY AND THE MOON.

Adapted from FROEBEL, *by* KATE S. KELLOGG. E. S.

From "Songs for Little Children," for the Kindergarten and Primary Schools, by Eleanor Smith. Publishers: Milton Bradley Co., Springfield, Mass.; Thos. Charles Co., Chicago. With permission of author and publishers.

O LOOK AT THE MOON.

MRS. FOLLEN. W. W. GILCHRIST.

About Waltz Time.

THE LITTLE MAIDEN AND THE STARS.

EMILY HUNTINGTON MILLER. GEORGE L. OSGOOD.

Moderato and Sweetly.

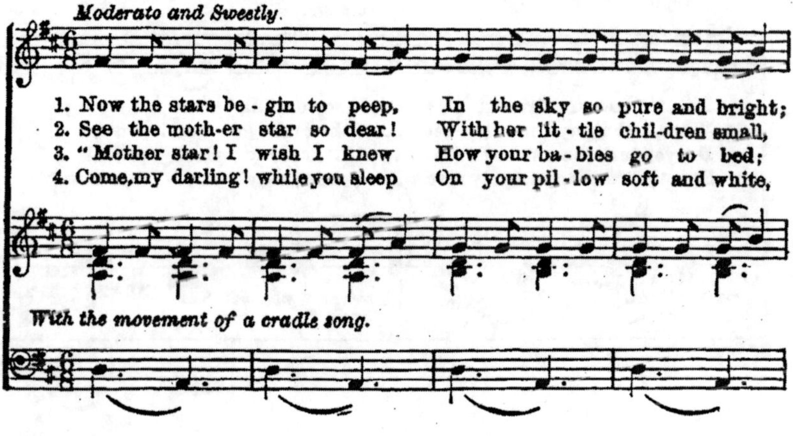

Ba - by soon must go to sleep, She must bid the stars good-night:
And the fa - ther watching near, Pret - ty stars! I love you all!
Do they run as chickens do, Hid - ing ev - 'ry yel - low head?
Stars will thro' your win-dow peep, Smiling, "Ba - by, dear, good-night!
Lit - tle feet are tired of play, Come, my dar - ling, come a - way!
When I shut my eyes to sleep, All the night your watch you keep;
Do you tuck them soft and deep In a fleec - y cloud to sleep?
Sweet-ly dreams and safe - ly rest In your pret - ty cra - dle nest!
poco cresc.
Lit - tle feet are tired of play, Come, my darling, come a - way!
When I shut my eyes to sleep, All the night your watch you keep.
Do you tuck them soft and deep, In a fleec - y cloud to sleep?
Sweetly dreams and safely rest In your pret-ty cra - dle nest!"
poco ritard.
a tempo.
poco rit.

THE CHILD AND THE STAR.

Andante con moto e tranquillo. J. W. Elliott.

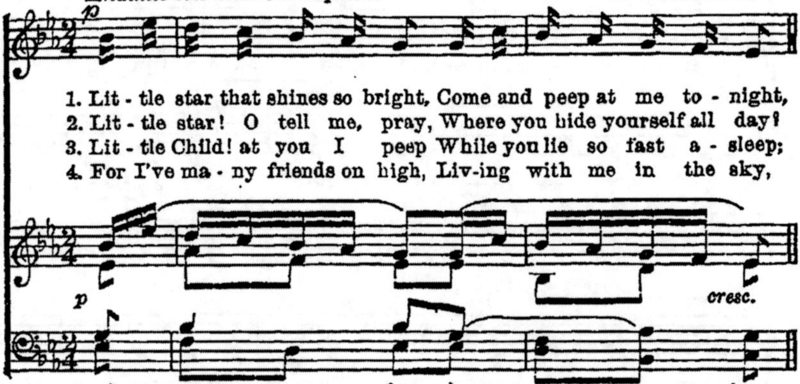

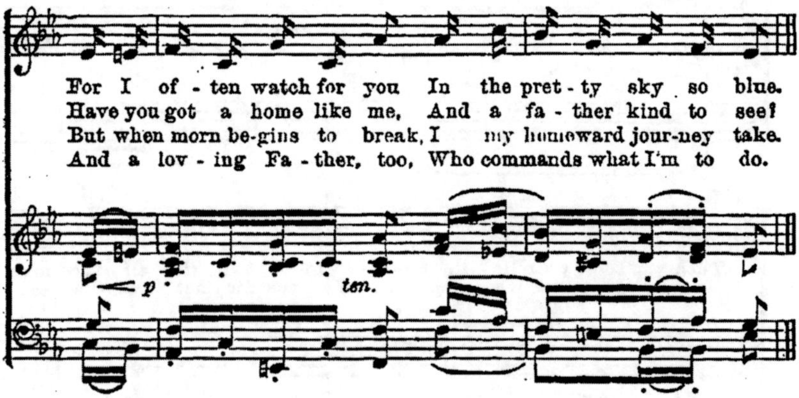

TWINKLE, TWINKLE LITTLE STAR.

Allegretto moderato. J. W. Elliott.

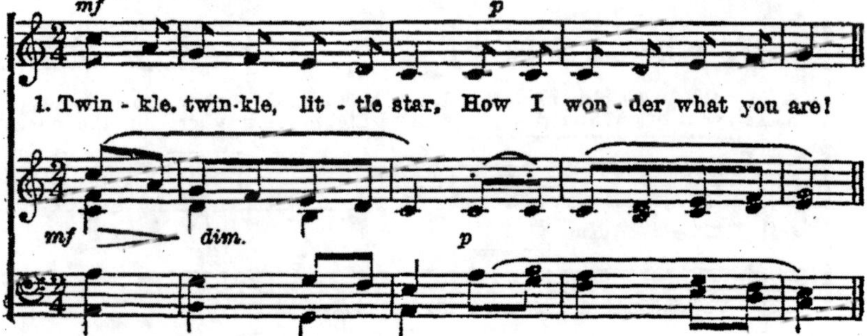

p
poco rit.
Up a - bove the world so high, Like a dia - mond in the sky.
p
f
fz
p poco rit.
mf
p
2. When the blaz - ing sun is gone, When he noth - ing shines up - on,
3. Then the trav - 'ler in the dark Thanks you for your ti - ny spark:
mf
dim.
p
p
poco rit.
Then you show your lit - tle light, Twin - kle, twin - kle, all the night.
How could he see where to go, If you did not twin - kle so?
p
f
fz
p pcoo rit.
mf
p
4. In the dark blue sky you keep, Oft - en through my curtains peep,
5. As your bright and ti - ny spark Lights the trav'ler in the dark.
mf
dim.
p

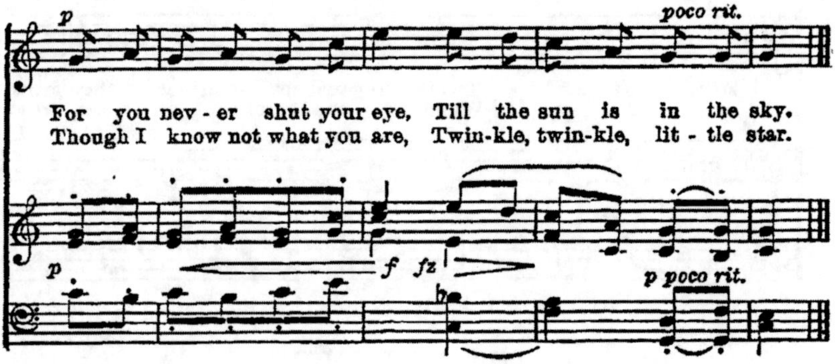

STARS AND DAISIES.

E. S.

From "Songs for Little Children," for the Kindergarten and Primary Schools, by Eleanor Smith. Publishers: Milton Bradley Co., Springfield, Mass.; Thos. Charles Co., Chicago. With permission of author and publishers.

THE LIGHT BIRD.

Arranged from ROBERT KOHL, *by* E. S.

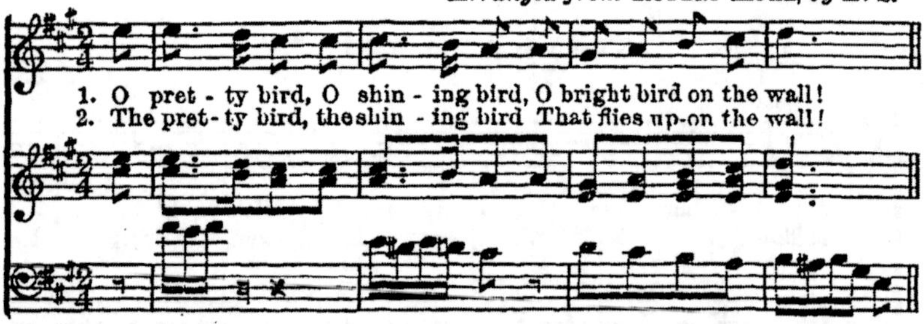

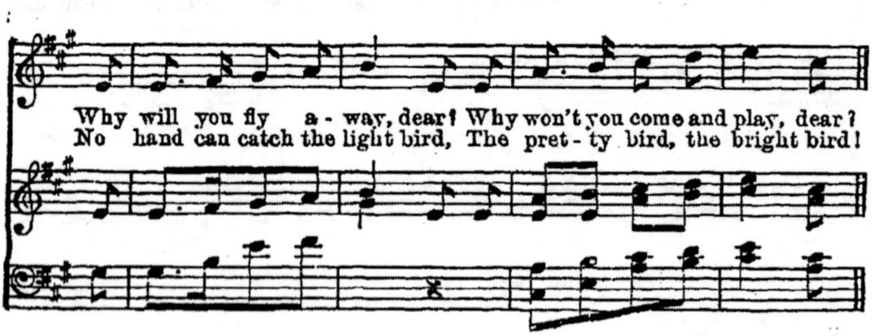

THE LIGHT BIRD.

ELIZABETH CHARLES LE BOURGEOIS. ELEANOR SMITH.

THE SHADOW RABBIT.

LAURA E. RICHARDS. *Child Song (Old French).*

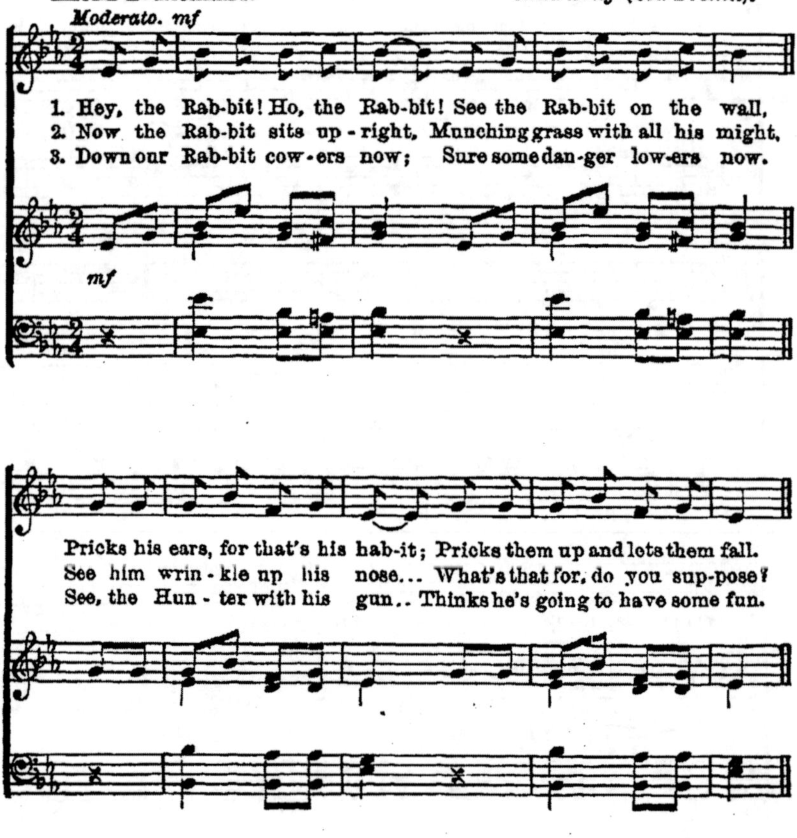

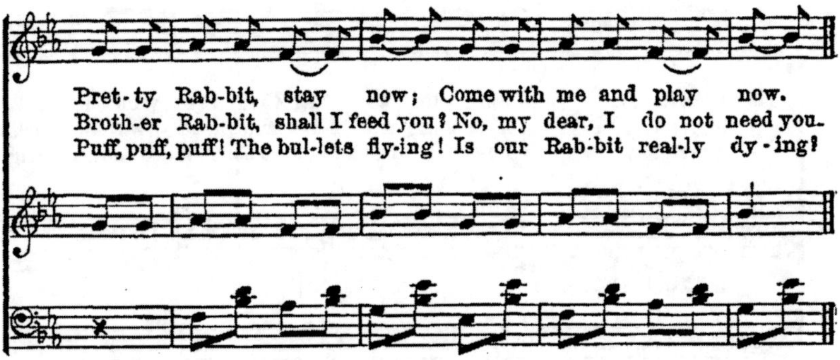

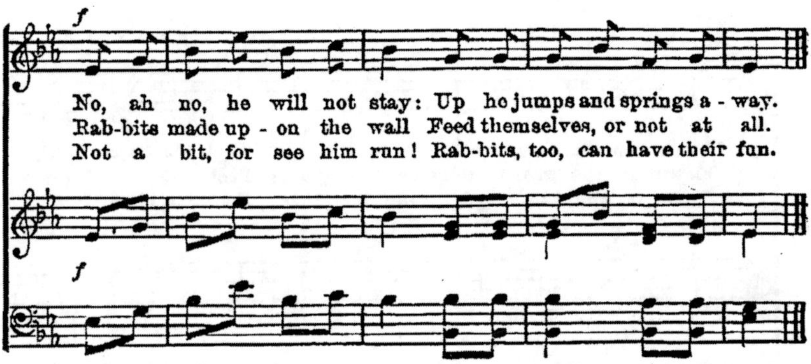

THE LITTLE WINDOW.

EMILY HUNTINGTON MILLER. W. W. GILCHRIST.

Briskly and gracefully.

light!...... Shin - ing so clear thro' my win - dow bright;
light!...... Mak - ing the fields and mead - ows so bright;
light!...... Love is the sun-shine that makes the heat bright;
Down from the sky, soft - ly you fly; Peek - a - boo light,
Flow'rs in the grass smile as you pass; Peek - a - boo light,
Pure we would be, shin - ing like thee; Peek - a - boo light,
beau - ti - ful light, Peek - a - boo, beau - ti - ful, beau-ti - ful light.
beau - ti - ful light, Peek - a - boo, beau - ti - ful, beau-ti - ful light.
beau - ti - ful light, Peek - a - boo, beau - ti - ful, beau-ti - ful light.

THE WINDOW.

GEORGE H. PAGE. ELEANOR SMITH.

TRANSFORMATION GAME.

EMILIE POULSSON. ELEANOR SMITH.

Moderato.

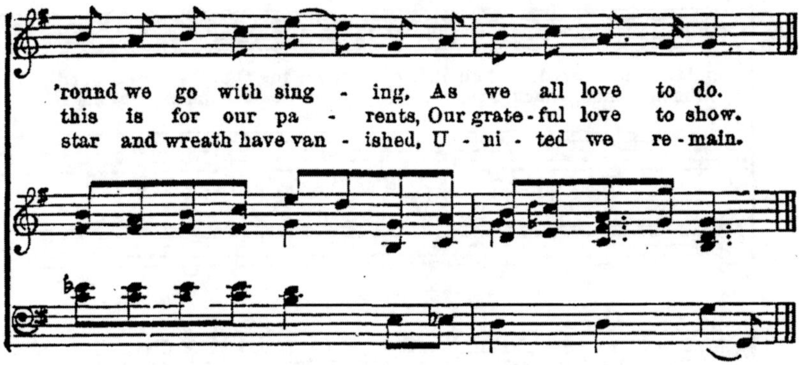

THE CHARCOAL-BURNER.

EMILY HUNTINGTON MILLER. FRED. FIELD BULLARD, Op. 30. No. 1.

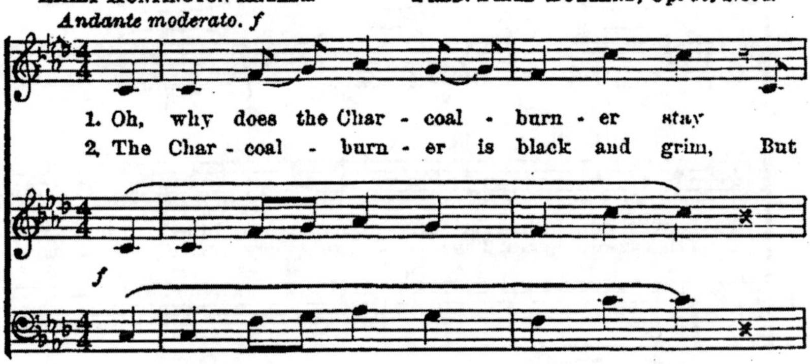

piles the wood, And burns it slow to the char-coal good. The
whack, whack, whack, And burns the wood to the char-coal black.
Blacksmith's hammer goes " Kling, klang, kling; Char-coal, char-coal
Knives and ax - es, shov-els and rakes, Shoes for the po - ny the
hur-ry and bring, For how can I shoe the po-ny's
Black-smith makes. The bel-lows blow and the ham-mers
feet, With - out good char-coal the iron to heat!
beat, But he must have char-coal the iron to heat.

THE CARPENTER.

EMILIE POULSSON. W. W. GILCHRIST.

THE CARPENTER.

EMILIE POULSSON. EUPHEMIA M. PARKER.
Arr. by F. F. BULLARD.

Con moto giojoso. mf

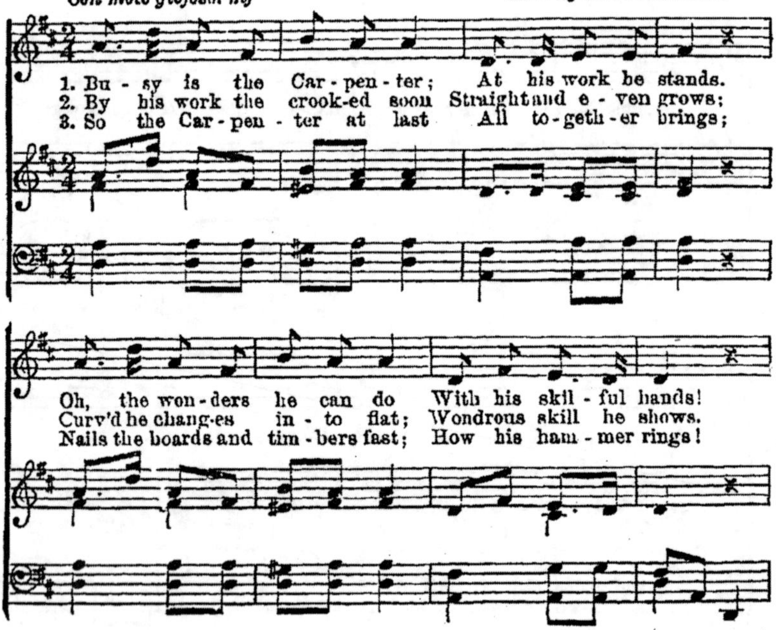

✽ These measures may be repeated ad lib. or omitted entirely.

THE BRIDGE.

EMILIE POULSSON. ELEANOR SMITH.

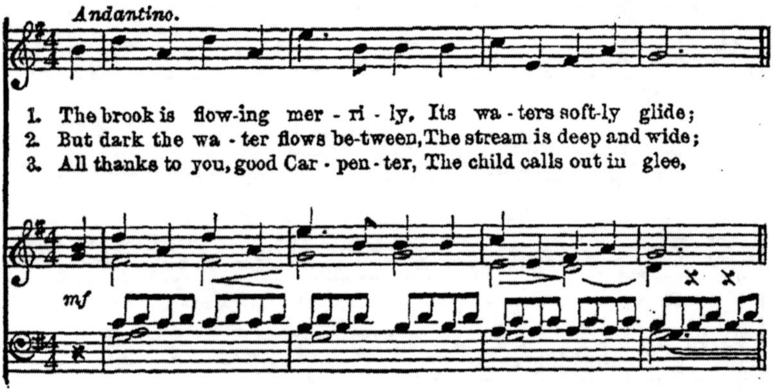

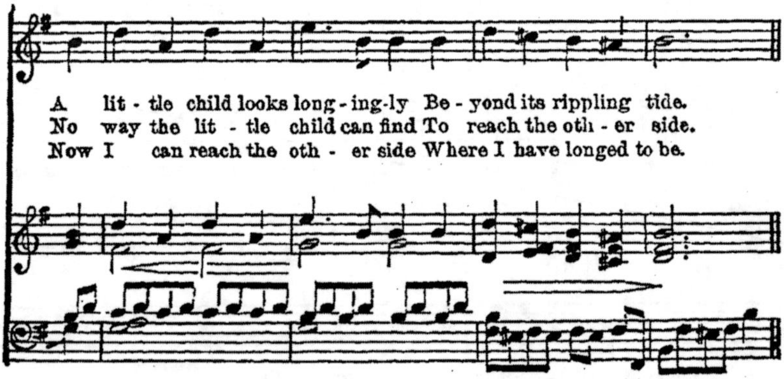

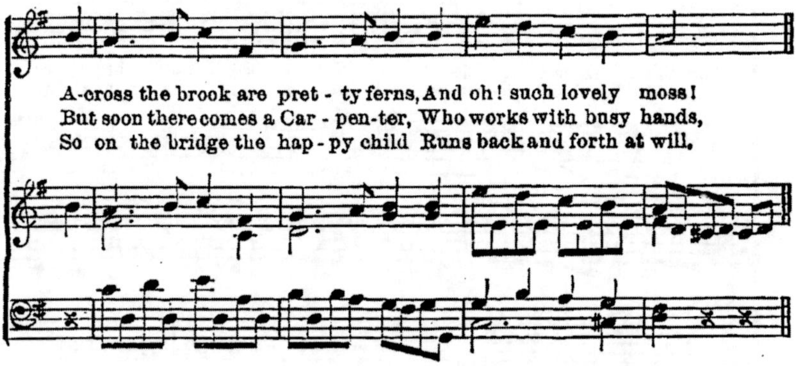

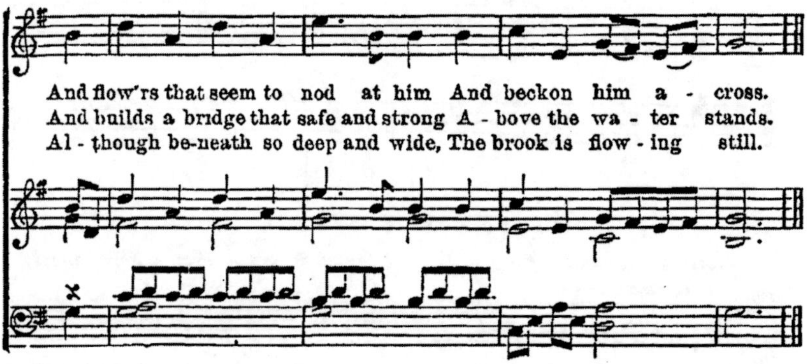

THE JOINER.

NORA A. SMITH. *Arranged from* ROBERT KOHL.

Andante non troppo. mf

THE FARMYARD.

CARO A. DUGAN. *Adapted from two French Folk Songs.*

* Imitate here the actual cries of the animals instead of using the syllables.

THE GARDEN-GATE.

EMILY HUNTINGTON MILLER. W. W. GILCHRIST.

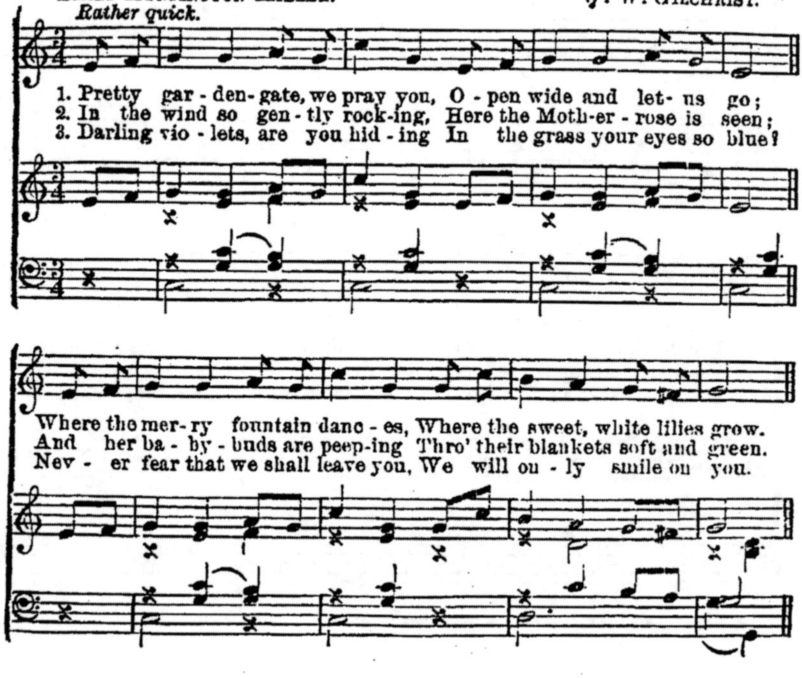

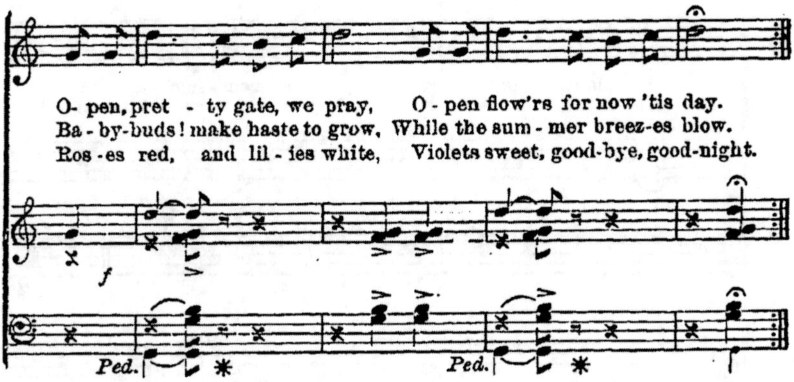

Last verse,—dying away.

THE LITTLE GARDENER.

LAURA E. RICHARDS. *Hungarian Folk Song.*

Tempo di Valse Lento.

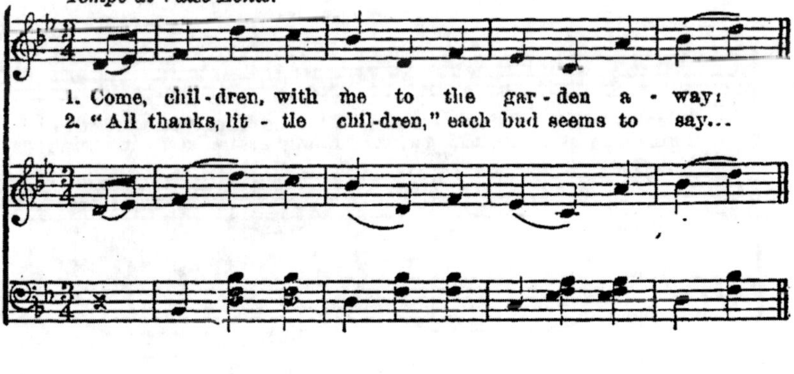

The plants are all wait - ing our com - ing to - day.
All thanks for the love that you show us to - day.
In heat and in sun - shine is droop-ing each leaf,...
Now beau - ty and per - fume shall bless you each one....
But the chil - dren are com - ing to bring them re - lief.
In.... lov - ing re - turn, for the good you have done.
Trinkle - trink! Trinkle - trink! How the drops chime and wink!
Twinkle-twink! Twinkle-twink! Now like stars see us wink!

THE LITTLE GARDENER.

KATE L. BROWN. CARL REINECKE.

LITTLE ANNIE'S GARDEN.

Mrs. Follen. Eleanor Smith.

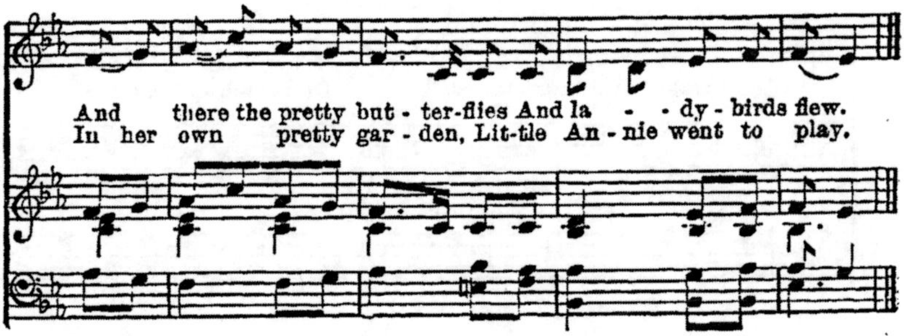

THE LITTLE PLANT.

KATE L. BROWN. W. W. GILCHRIST.

Smoothly, and moderately slow.

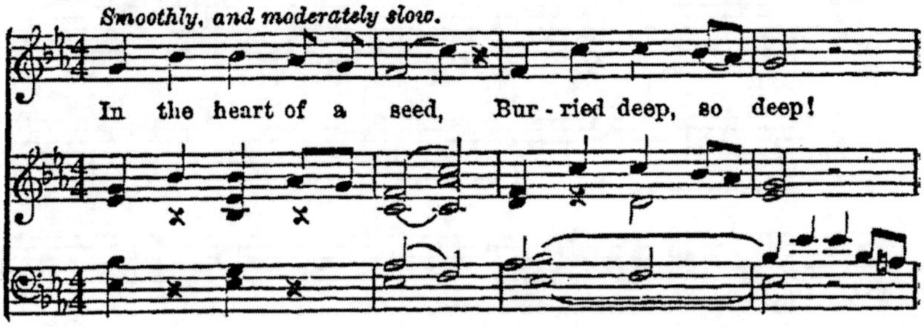

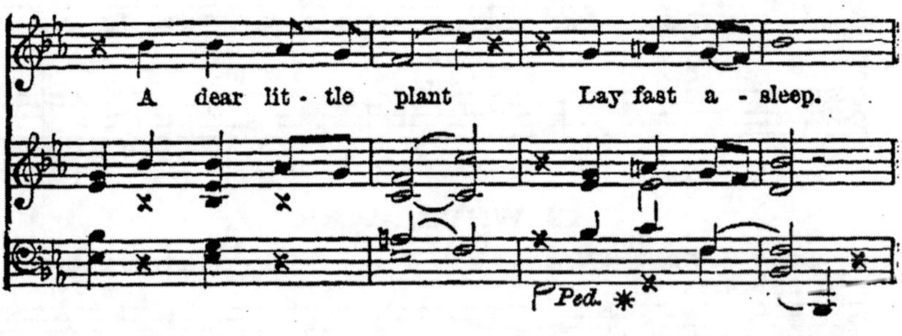

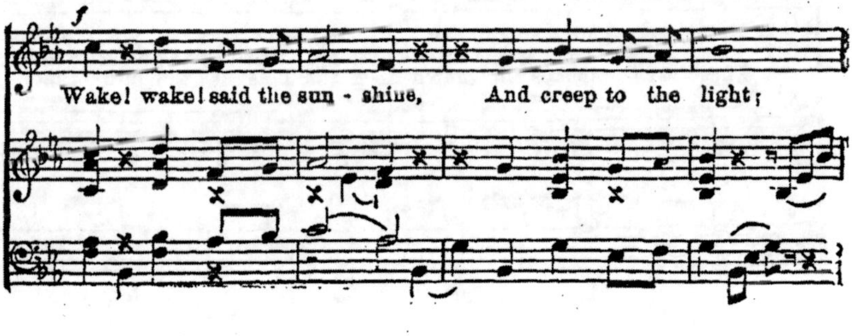

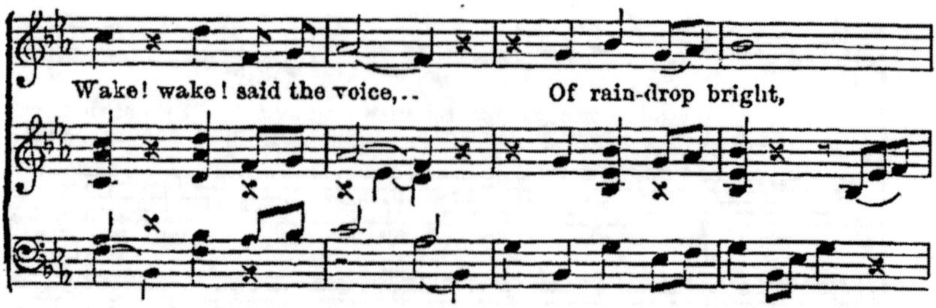

THE WHEEL-WRIGHT.

EMILY HUNTINGTON MILLER. ELEANOR SMITH.

Moderato.

Wheel-wright's shop. Wheel-wright! show us the way you do,
hands so strong, Straight and stead - y the au - ger goes, And
holds them tight, This is the rim of i - ron and wood, To
Mak - ing the wheel so round and true, Turn - ing fast and
smooth and true the hole it.. grows, Turn - ing stead - y and
fin - ish my wheel so use - ful and good, Turn - ing fast and
FINE.
turning slow, This is the way the wheel must go.
turning slow, This is the way the auger must go.
turning slow, This is the way the wheel must go.

THE KNIGHTS AND THE GOOD CHILD.

EMILY HUNTINGTON MILLER. ELEANOR SMITH.

ride to find The child that is lov - ing and good and kind."
"This is the child so dear, Brave Knights, you see him here!"
O child, be al - ways good and gay!
a tempo.
Then gal - lop, and gal - lop, and gal - lop a - way.

THE KNIGHTS AND THE BAD CHILD.

EMILY HUNTINGTON MILLER. ELEANOR SMITH.

Allegretto marcato.

Adagio.
vis - it the hap - py chil-dren's land? Ah, brave knights you will
Adagio.
all be sad To know that my child is self - ish and bad.
It grieves me much to say....... He can - not ride to -
day;...... On - ly good chil - dren with us can go, Then a -

THE KNIGHTS AND THE MOTHER.

EMILY HUNTINGTON MILLER. E. S.

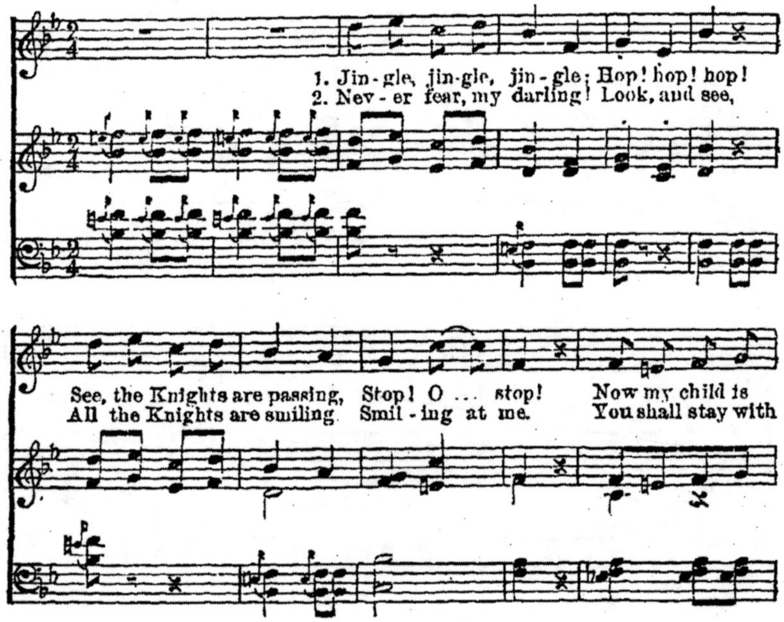

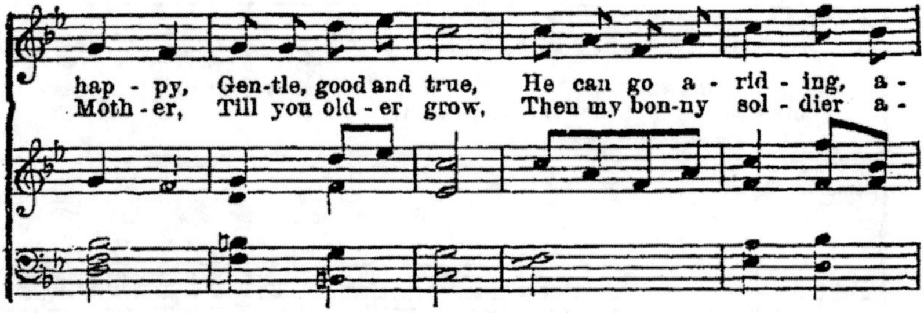

THE KNIGHTS AND THE MOTHER.

EMILY HUNTINGTON MILLER. ELEANOR SMITH.

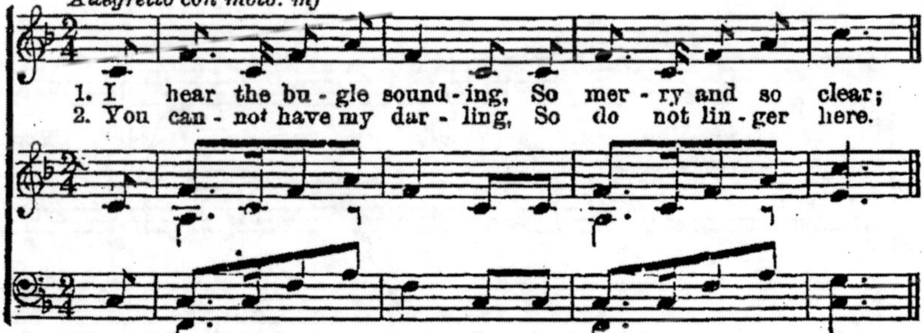

The knights come gai-ly rid - ing, They want thee, child, I fear.
Safe in my heart I'll keep him, He is so good and dear.
pp
Now hide thee quick, my dar - - ling, And nes - tle close to me,
Now do not tar - ry lon - ger, But swift - ly ride a - way;
p
cresc.
For not one dim - pled fin - ger The gal - lant knights shall see.
Peep out and smile, my lad - die, And bid the knights good-day.
f
Jin - gle, jin - gle, jin - gle, O - ver hill and dell, You

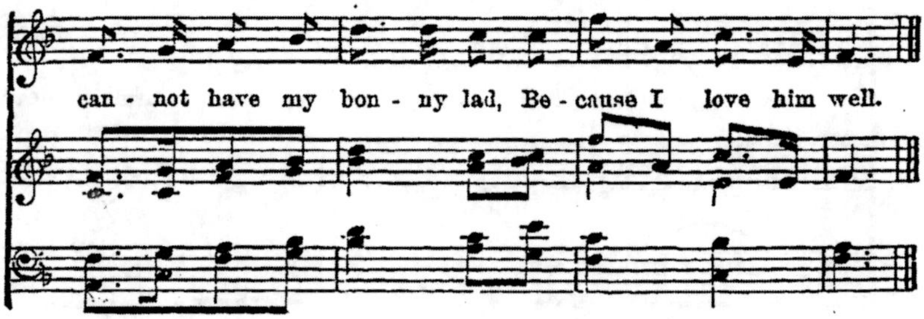

HIDE AND SEEK.

HENRIETTA R. ELIOT. *After* HAYDN, *by* F. F. BULLARD.

Andante con moto.

CUCKOO.

HENRIETTA R. ELIOT. FRED. FIELD BULLARD, Op. 30, No. 2.

Molto moderato, p dolce.

HIDING GAME.

KATE L. BROWN. CARL REINECKE.

GUESSING THE SINGER.

KATE L. BROWN. (*Swabian Popular Song.*) CARL REINECKE.

THE CHURCH.

LAURA E. RICHARDS. ELEANOR SMITH.

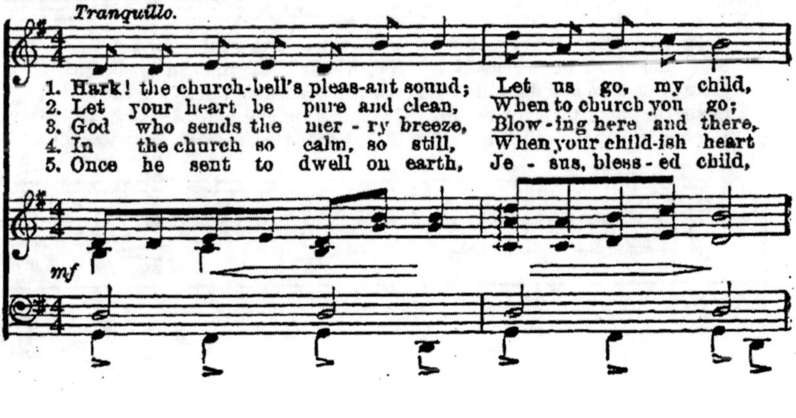

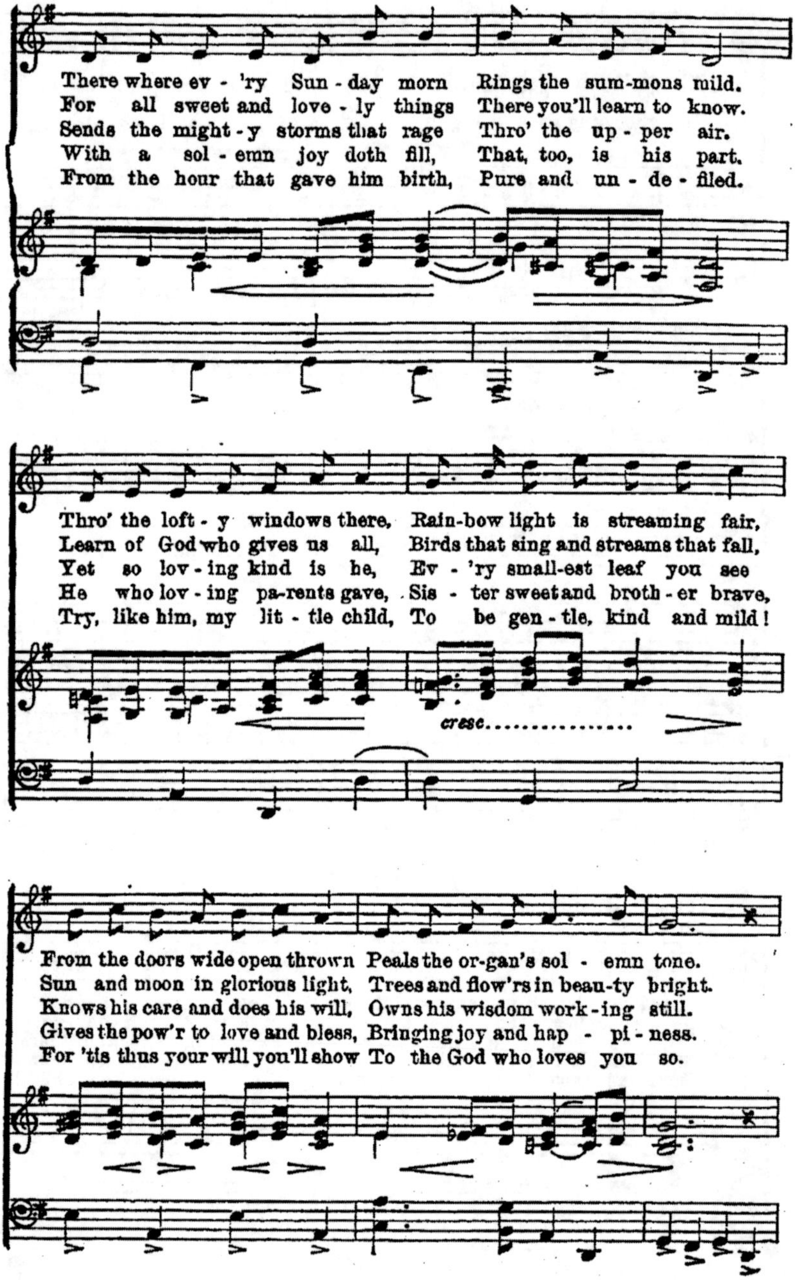
There where ev - 'ry Sun - day morn Rings the sum-mons mild.
For all sweet and love - ly things There you'll learn to know.
Sends the might - y storms that rage Thro' the up - per air.
With a sol - emn joy doth fill, That, too, is his part.
From the hour that gave him birth, Pure and un - de - filed.
Thro' the loft - y windows there, Rain-bow light is streaming fair,
Learn of God who gives us all, Birds that sing and streams that fall,
Yet so lov - ing kind is he, Ev - 'ry small-est leaf you see
He who lov - ing pa-rents gave, Sis - ter sweet and broth - er brave,
Try, like him, my lit - tle child, To be gen - tle, kind and mild!
cresc.
From the doors wide open thrown Peals the or-gan's sol - emn tone.
Sun and moon in glorious light, Trees and flow'rs in beau-ty bright.
Knows his care and does his will, Owns his wisdom work - ing still.
Gives the pow'r to love and bless, Bringing joy and hap - pi - ness.
For 'tis thus your will you'll show To the God who loves you so.

WANDERING SONG.

KATE L. BROWN. *After an Old French Lullaby.*

Allegretto. mf Dolce.

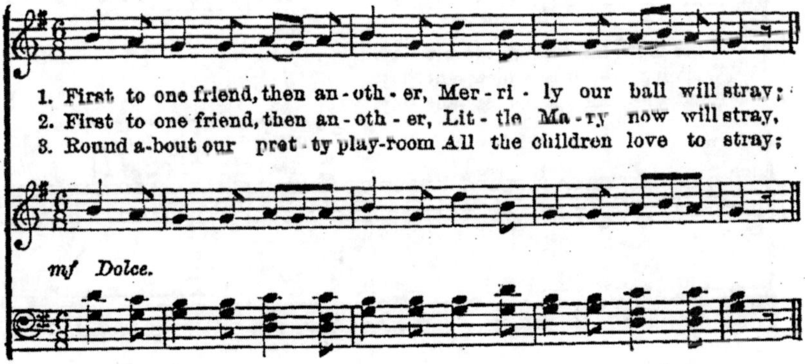

On it goes a-mong the children, Hap-py com-rade in their play;
She will vis - it with the children, Hap-py com-rade in their play;
Sing-ing wel-come to the sunshine, Gold-en sunshine on its way;
Wishing one and then an-oth-er, Wishing all a pleas-ant day,
Wishing one and then an-oth-er, Wishing all a pleas-ant day,
Wishing pictures, birds and flow-ers, Each and all a pleas-ant day,
Wish-ing all a pleas-ant day.
Wish-ing all a pleas-ant day.
Each and all a pleas-ant day.
p

THE VISIT.

KATE L. BROWN. *From "Childrens' Songs."*

Allegro Commodo. f CARL REINECKE.

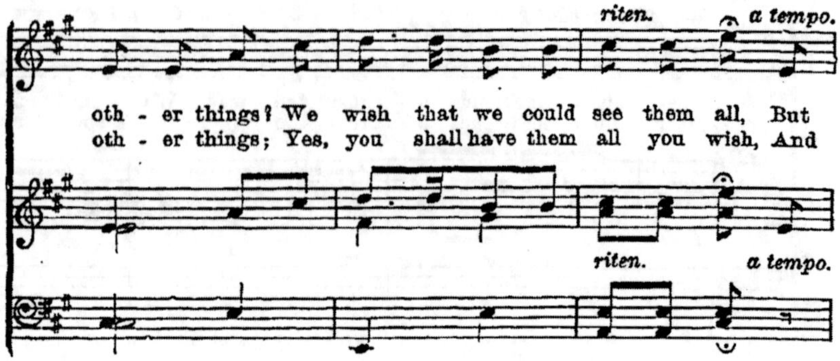

THE WANDERING SONG.

NORA A. SMITH. FRED. FIELD BULLARD.

Allegro non troppo. mf Op. 30, No. 7.

When first the buds be - gin to peep, And birds be - gin to sing:
And hear the whis-per of the grass, The in-sects' sleep - y hum:
When beeches wave their yel - low flags And scar - let ma - ples blaze;
When all the i - cy streams are still, And mer-ry sleigh-bells chime:
p
cresc.
The lamb-kins frol - ic in the field, The ba - by leaves un-fold,
Tne ros - es bloom on ev - 'ry side, The wheat is grow - ing high,
The squirrel's stor - ing up his nuts, The corn is gath - er'd in,
The skat - ers skim a - cross the pond, The north-wind whistles free,
p
cresc
f
dim.
p
And dan - de - li - ons from the grass Shine out like stars of gold.
And lil - ies blos-som white and gold Where qui-et wa - ters lie....
And ro sy ap - ples, smooth and ripe, Fill up the farm-er's bin.
And in the si - lent for - est waits The dar-ling Christmas Tree.
f
dim.
p

REFRAIN. *f ma dolce.*

RIPPLING, PURLING LITTLE RIVER.

W. W. GILCHRIST.

From "*Children's Songs, and How to Sing them.*" With permission of W. L. Tomlins.

flow - ing, hast - 'ning on! See the spark - ling,
sil - ver rip - ples, As they van - ish, one by one;
Down the hill - side, thro' the val - ley, Slid - ing
soft - ly, mur - m'ring low,.... Wa - t'ring flow - ers,

rall.
turn - ing mill-wheels, Giv - ing joy wher - e'er you go.
rall.
a tempo.
Down the hill - side, thro' the val - ley, Slid - ing soft - ly,
a tempo.
mur-m'ring low, Wa - t'ring flow - ers, turn - ing mill-wheels,
Giv - ing joy wher - e'er you go.

INDEX OF FIRST LINES.

THE END.